DESIGNING
ECOMMERCE
WEBSITES

A UX DESIGN HANDBOOK FOR
GREAT ONLINE SHOPS

TRANSMITTER PRESS

This edition published in Great Britain in 2019 by
Transmitter Press
Copyright © Matt Isherwood 2017, 2019

ISBN 978-0-9957313-2-5

ABOUT THE AUTHOR

Matt Isherwood is a UX consultant who uses evidence to help ecommerce sites improve their design. He specialises in working with growing startups. He has over 10 years professional experience in design, starting his career at the BBC, before being the lead UX designer at onefinestay. He taught workshops and courses at General Assembly for four years and now carries out workshops for companies.

He writes regularly about UX and can be found at **mattish.com**

Ecommerce is massive. There are over 1.66bn online buyers worldwide—a number that is constantly growing (source: go.mattish.com/ecom0a). **However in Q3 of 2018 the global conversion rate was at 2.42%** (source: go.mattish.com/ecom0b), **lower than it had been for the past year. It shows just how much room there still is to help users become customers. The easiest way to do it is not to slash prices or harass users with promotions but by improving the design to create a smoother shopping experience.**

One ecommerce site that I worked on a few years ago illustrates how design is about more than polished graphics. Like most of my projects, before designing I first set up user testing to see what users thought of the site. Their products were great and the visual design and imagery were beautiful. Users were immediately impressed and said how excited they were.

However the filters were fiddly, the product pages weren't clearly laid out, and when it came to making a purchase, users got stuck. They weren't sure how products were priced or how to select different options. If they did work this out it then wasn't clear how to change things, so they'd have to start all over again. The initial great impression had totally worn off.

It didn't matter that they had the best-looking products in the world, with sharp type and colour combinations, as users were tripping up on the essential functions. Many times I've seen user experience (or UX) most defined by the frustration of things not working as people expect. Of course there's room to innovate and delight but doing so without the core functions performing only makes things worse.

If your site is a vehicle then this book is here to help you get the engine running smoothly before you move onto the paint job.

WHO THIS BOOK IS FOR

This book has been designed to be accessible to a wide range of people who are involved in selling online. It is applicable to any site that follows the ecommerce funnel, regardless of the sector you work in (more on that funnel coming up).

This book isn't just for designers as there are plenty of roles that influence the design process. I've tried to avoid any UX jargon and requiring too much prior knowledge, so the likes of marketers, developers, and startup founders can dip in and out. If there's anything you don't understand, I've put a glossary of the few technical terms at the back.

The advice here is device-agnostic and every guideline can apply to desktop, tablet, and mobile (other than in a couple of places, where it is flagged). With mobile users forming the bulk of ecommerce traffic, modern websites must work well on all sizes of screen.

WHY LISTEN TO ME?

I'm a UX designer with over 10 years experience, more than seven of which have been in the ecommerce space. I've worked with a range of companies selling a variety of products, including three and a half years at one rapid growth travel startup (onefinestay) and four years of freelance consulting.

I've taught this subject since 2013 too. I initially developed a lot of the advice in this book through teaching regular workshops at General Assembly in London where it proved to be robust and applicable to a wide variety of people. Over the years since I've written pretty solidly, with weekly blogs on UX design, including popular articles on the likes of UX Planet and the InVision blog.

I've learned the advice here over the course of my career and they are the principles I apply when I'm hired as a UX consultant. I've designed ecommerce sites; I've researched many websites in this space; I've looked at a lot of analytics; I've analysed many user tests; and not to mention I've shopped on plenty myself.

Even as someone with experience, I think you should be wary of people offering 'best practice', as there will always be cases where it can be challenged. This is why I refer to this content as guidelines rather than hard and fast rules, but where possible I explain the data or experience that has led to my conclusions.

THE ECOMMERCE FUNNEL - HOW THIS BOOK IS STRUCTURED

The five chapters in this book are organised to mirror the structure of the vast majority of ecommerce websites. This structure consists of types of page that exist not just due to convention: they exist because there are jobs that a user needs to do on every website. It's known as a funnel because there are always more people entering at the top, tapering off to the few that purchase at the bottom.

LANDING

The landing pages are the equivalent of the shop window in a physical store and their job is to show users what the site offers and encourage them to enter the store. The advice here looks at how you can get your message across quickly and get users to hang around longer.

LISTINGS

This is similar to the inside layout of the store and the aim is to help users compare different options to find something they want to buy. These guidelines cover both the structure of the page itself and what can live on each listing.

LANDING

LISTINGS

PRODUCT

CHECKOUT

MORE

PRODUCT

The product pages do the job of a product's packaging in a real-life store. It needs to show off the thing despite users not being able to experience it, and must convey all the information users need to know to be confident in making a purchase. These guidelines take you through what you need to have on a product page to increase a user's likelihood of buying.

CHECKOUT

This is where the user comes to pay and often organise delivery. It's a pretty standardised process so this advice will explain the conventions and also things you can do to make it more convenient for the user to give you their money. There are a few guidelines in this chapter that cover the basket page too.

MORE

Finally there's a chapter for content that doesn't fit in the main ecommerce funnel. These include principles that apply to the website as a whole and a few other page types worth mentioning.

• • •

When starting out, not all sites will require every step of the funnel. For example, if you're selling a single product then it's possible to just have a product page and checkout, while if you're only selling a few products you probably don't need the listings functionality.

This book is designed so that you can easily find what you need, with a guideline per webpage element. Some of the guidelines (on the grey pages) are framed as questions and they pose things to think about that may not apply to all sites. Overall this book doesn't aim to be a theoretical tome but a handbook that is easy to pick up and use, so it can answer your challenges as they arise.

Within the chapters each guideline is presented on a double-page spread, and most of them come with an illustration to help clarify the meaning. These illustrations are in an outline, wireframe style to demonstrate the concept without extraneous detail. The illustration dimensions are similar to mobile screen sizes as most ecommerce traffic now comes from these devices.

The thing about good UX design advice is that when explained it sounds like common sense. Yet it's amazing how often I still see sites that don't do even the most obvious things. I hope you're already following some of the guidelines here but chances are there are some that will be new.

ABOUT THE SECOND EDITION

This is the second edition of this book or, as I like to think of it, the 'complete' edition. Being someone who has spent most of their career working in the web, I saw the first edition as something of a 'beta' release, which I've iterated on to make a much more polished 2.0 release. There are three main ways the book has been improved:

— Every single word has been considered and most of the content has been either rewritten or rephrased around specific design elements, to make the concepts more robust.

— There are 15 new guidelines in this book (whilst three have been removed or merged) to cover more parts of ecommerce websites.

— Every guideline now comes with a further reading link, so you can learn more about the area in question, or find data that backs up statements in the guidelines. Several of these lead to articles I've written where I expand on that topic.

I hope the book will be useful as a comprehensive beginner's guide and as a jumping off point to learn more about ecommerce UX design. Please do build on the advice as you learn more, and test the specifics with your own site and audience.

DESIGNING ECOMMERCE WEBSITES

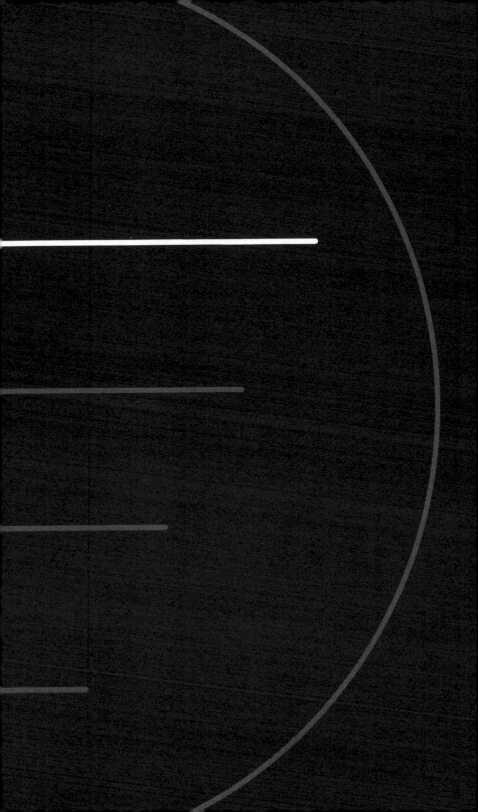

LANDING

In reality any page can be a landing page, as in web analytics terms it simply describes the location that users enter the site. However most websites create pages specifically designed for a user's introductory experience. In ecommerce it's no different and that's the type we'll be focussing on here.

A good site thinks about where the users are coming from and presents them with a page that recognises they will have a few key questions that need answering. In the early days of a website the homepage will be the dominant landing page for the majority of users.

As websites grow and marketing effort intensifies it becomes useful to have specific landing pages for certain campaigns. This is particularly important for paid search where the page and headings need to match the keywords that people have been searching for, or users won't think the content is relevant for their needs.

Be it a homepage or a campaign landing page, the requirements are the same.

REQUIREMENTS

As this represents the top of your funnel—in traditional retail terms think of it as your shop window—you need to consider the first impression you give for your website and company.

You need to tell people what you offer and why you're different and you need to do it quickly. New users are fast to bounce if they don't see the benefit of what you offer: very few people have the patience to hang around when they don't immediately understand it.

In particular they need to understand how buying from you is better than buying something similar from a site like

Amazon, where they probably already have an account. Their commitment to you is low at this stage.

You also need to show and prove to your users that you are of sufficient quality to be trusted. Only the companies with big marketing budgets and well-established brands can dodge this requirement.

SUCCESS

Landing pages have a very clear metric for success. They succeed by pushing people deeper into the site, usually onto listings pages, so this is the main conversion rate to watch.

Pretty much any other metric is a distraction. A low bounce rate is good for all landing pages as you don't want users leaving but this comes second to users going to the next step in your funnel. Having a clarity of purpose makes designing easier as everything you do can be measured against a goal.

The concept of attention ratio is useful here too. This ratio is defined by the number of links on the page against the number of primary actions you want them to take (which should always be one). An ideal page would have a ratio of 1:1 (one page with one link to the goal). Practical considerations mean you'll almost certainly need a few more links, but the aim should be to keep that ratio as close to 1:1 as possible.

If you're getting to a ratio of 30:1 or 40:1 this means there is big room for improvement. All these extra links are distractions from the main thing you want users to do, and add cognitive load to their visit.

The guidelines in this chapter will delve into how you can focus your users attention and get those clicks (or taps) in the direction you want.

MAIN IMAGE

Let's start at the top. What's the first thing people will notice about your website? Keep in mind they aren't likely to spend long looking.

It's almost certainly going to be an image. Our minds process pictures quicker than any words, so you need to consider if your main image is working hard enough to give the impression you want.

If you're in any doubt you should use this space to show what it is that you sell. Help people know they are in the right place, and don't let them feel uncertain. This could be as simple as product shots, or it could show your target audience, or it could follow established styles in your sector.

There are lots of details coded into every image, so make sure yours use the right ones. If a fashion site has an image of a middle-aged woman attending a classy event in a city then you instantly understand the intended gender, age, location, and income demographics of the target audience. If the site had a photo of a man in his 20s with a beard, sat at a rustic-looking cafe, you would understand this is aimed at a very different set of people.

Users make their minds up about a website in 0.05 seconds, and other stats **go.mattish.com/ecom1**

WHAT'S THE FIRST THING

PEOPLE WILL NOTICE ABOUT YOUR WEBSITE?

MAIN HEADING

If users have arrived at your website and you've made it clear what you sell through your imagery, what should you use your heading text for?

You could spell out what you sell further. You could jump into special offers or promote new products. In fact there's a more important thing to cover first: how your site differs from others.

This is typically known as your Unique Selling Point (USP). If you fail to explain this, what reason do people have to stay on your site? Why not just go to Amazon, eBay, Booking.com or another big market place where they've already got an account? Your difference should be something that marks you out as special and shouldn't be something that others can easily offer. Priding yourself on things like free shipping and free returns just won't cut it.

Your USP should ideally focus on just one thing. Don't muddy the waters and present three or four things. Once you've got it worked out, you should be able to convey this thing in only a few words so you can tell users straight away. Good examples can be niches ("we specialise in this product type") or special services ("free personalisation of products") or in how the product/service is produced ("no sweats shops, eco-friendly etc").

Be careful not to get too clever in your wording so you leave people guessing: inventing words, hashtags, and using internal jargon can all lead to this kind of confusion.

📖 Examples of small websites that get the top of their homepage right
go.mattish.com/ecom2

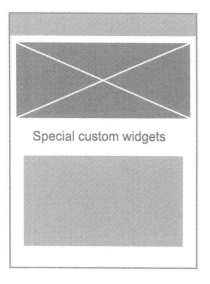

Special custom widgets

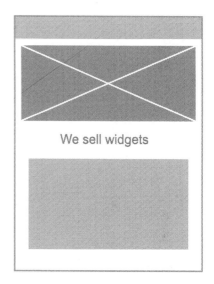

We sell widgets

CAROUSELS

Carousels are a useful feature for fitting lots of content on a page, as they allow the user to rotate through different items. They're common on ecommerce websites, particularly big department stores that have lots of products.

Over the years there's been a backlash against them in the UX community. This is because they hide content from users and as a result most of it doesn't get clicked on. The analytics I've seen on sites that use them bear this out. However, there is a way that carousels can be effective: when all the content works together.

On desktop you can use a carousel to act like a mini video. It should auto-play through the slides because users tend not to click themselves. The slides should be mostly images as users won't have time to read anything in detail.

Think about how the images combine to show the different elements of what you offer. If you're selling something that isn't easily explained in one image, then several can show things more clearly. A rule of thumb for carousels is that four slides is probably enough—any more and the final ones are going to be missed as users scroll past and down the page.

When it comes to mobile, the autoplaying carousel is too fiddly and should be avoided. Either show all of the slides in a column down the page or just show the most important one.

A few more thoughts about using carousels effectively
go.mattish.com/ecom3

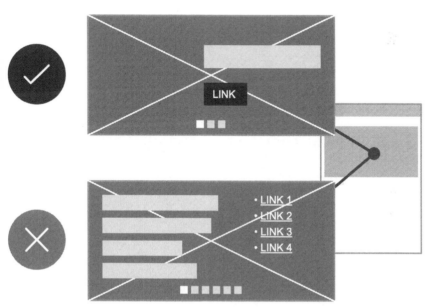

PRIMARY BUTTON

It's easy for homepages and landing pages to get carried away explaining a brand to users and showing off lots of products but if you're not careful your content can actually distract from the core purpose of the page. It's a good idea to take a step back and ask yourself, "if I've not been to this site before, is it clear what I should do next?"

For ecommerce landing pages the aim should be getting users to take the next step in buying, which usually means browsing for products. There should be an obvious link or button to do this with text featuring a clear call to action (CTA) like 'shop'.

To help it stand out, use a bright, contrasting colour that is sparingly used—ideally just for the primary button on each page. This applies whether the button is on its own or part of a simple form, such as one on a travel site that asks for location and dates. For emphasis and usability it's also a good idea to make it nice and easy to click/tap, so don't make it too small.

How to design effective landing page buttons, with plenty of examples
go.mattish.com/ecom4

SHOP NOW

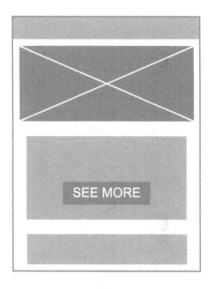

SEE MORE

REPEATED CTAS

You've identified the most important action you want users to take on the page. You've created your primary call to action button. Now you want to make sure users follow it—should you repeat the button?

A lot of websites at this point go with yes. They repeat their primary button several times down the page. The thinking being that they want to drive people there, so they had better make sure users don't miss it.

This isn't a great idea. With every extra link you're creating more things for the users to take in and understand—each repeated link increases the complexity and attention ratio of your page. On top of this, if there are lots of similar links on the page then the user is going to wonder which is the 'right' one or the one they should visit first. If there's a search button at the top, middle, and bottom of the page, they can only pick one but could be left wondering if they should have gone for another.

With repeated CTAs your primary action can end up competing against itself. I understand the temptation to try and increase click-throughs but you're much better off simplifying your homepage and constructing a single clear primary button that users can't miss.

More on how duplicate links make your site harder to use
go.mattish.com/ecom5

SHOP NOW

LEARN MORE

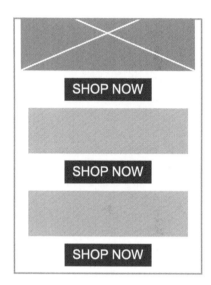

SHOP NOW

SHOP NOW

SHOP NOW

PRESS LOGOS

One thing we're probably all used to seeing when looking at website landing pages is rows of logos showing media and publications that have given the company press coverage. They're on most websites so do people really care about them? Aren't they just ignored now?

The answer is that most people really do notice them and care. Especially if you're a website that isn't a household name.

In every user test that I've run where press logos feature on the landing page, about 40% of users will notice them and state that they are reassured by their presence. It might seem like the oldest sales technique in the book but when presented with something completely new, seeing trusted names really does give users a layer of security.

If you've been lucky enough or worked hard to get good press coverage then don't forget to show users these quotes and publication logos early in the user's journey. It might just make the difference between whether they give you more attention or go back to a site they've used before.

📖 Press coverage or not, here's a detailed look at all the types of social proof you can use **go.mattish.com/ecom6**

TRUSTED NAMES

GIVE USERS A LAYER OF SECURITY

PROMOTIONS

Now you've got people to your site and to scroll down the page, there's lots you'll want to show them. Understandably you're going to want to promote and sell your products.

It might seem counter-intuitive but resist the temptation to fill the page with images of all products on sale, special offers, and big brand promises. You're effectively using your own content to compete against each other for your users' attention. Department store websites tend to do this a lot.

Having content that acts like advertising and 'shouts' at users to visit their bit of the site can look a lot like banner ads. Using this style will likely be counter-productive as users are well-attuned to ignoring advertising content.

You have the user on your site now, you can be more relaxed and help the user find what they're after rather than competing for their interest. Promotions are more powerful if they're rarely used, so try and only show one at a time.

This research shows that users ignore any content that looks like advertising **go.mattish.com/ecom7**

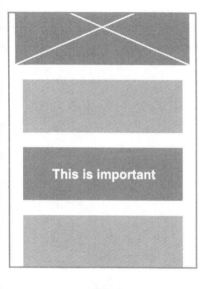

This is important

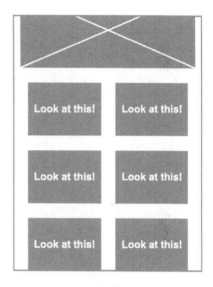

SHOULD YOU SHOW PRODUCTS OR NOT?

One question that comes up a lot when designing ecommerce sites is how many products to put on the homepage. Managers or merchandising folk are often keen to get products on there that they want to push, in the belief it will drive users through to these pages and increase sales. Unfortunately this isn't always the case and for big sites this can be a premature time to do it.

If you're a site with hundreds of products then what are the chances the user landing on your page will immediately want the small selection of products you've put there? Pretty low. In fact you could be confusing them into thinking this is all you offer, ending up with a few products that aren't representative of your store offering. Even if they do click-through, they may not like the product and can exit your site without getting a sense of the range of products you have available.

If you have a big website with lots of products, you should prioritise showing your product categories on the home page to give an overview of what you offer, with the aim of driving users through to your listings pages. If you are going to show products make sure it's with a focus on a few that are new or on special offer. Piling up lots of products only worsens the attention ratio.

For small sites (with fewer than about 20 products) it makes sense to show the products on your homepage. At this size categories are going to be overkill and these few products *are* your offering.

📖 Details about the dangers of leading with products on the homepage go.mattish.com/ecom8

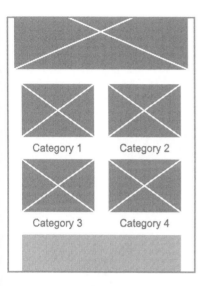

Category 1   Category 2

Category 3   Category 4

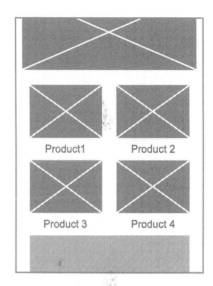

Product1   Product 2

Product 3   Product 4

VIDEO

The landing page is a place to impress. A lot of websites put money into high-end photography and some go further with short videos that show off products or tell the brand story.

No matter how flashy your video, if you put it on a landing page with the user needing to click play, be prepared for most people to ignore it. In the many user tests I've watched, this is the most common behaviour I've seen with landing page videos.

Why? At this stage of the user journey, their attention spans are short. Users are much more likely to decide to leave the site altogether and bounce, rather than stopping and committing time to watching something unknown.

Videos can become very useful later in the journey for explaining things like product features, when the user is more interested (see page 88). At the start you're better off helping the user to move through quickly so stick to short, auto-playing, looped videos.

A few more reasons why people don't watch your videos
go.mattish.com/ecom9

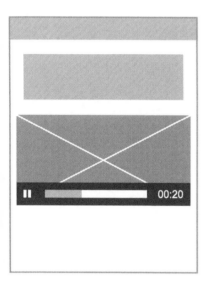

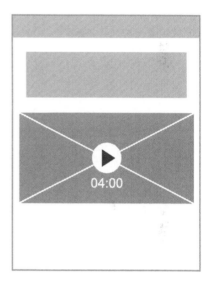

EXTRA CONTENT

You've done the hard marketing work in getting users onto your landing page and they seem to be interested. There's lots you could tell them about your company so now's the chance to get it all on there right?

Be careful. The longer you make your landing page the more you risk the user switching off or getting confused. Whilst users are happy to scroll, they'll soon stop if the content isn't directly related to their task.

Whenever you design, stick to the rule of 'one page, one purpose'. The purpose of this page is to introduce what you sell, and get the user to look for those products. Do they really need to know all about the history of your company, see five most recent blog posts, your latest tweets, and a wall of Instagram images? Social posts are particularly unhelpful as you've just got users onto your page and clicking these will take them away again.

The more things you put on the page, the more distractions you're giving the user from your main action and the key thing you really want them to do. If you have a lot of nuance to explain about how your store works, don't throw all the details at your users straight away, consider progressively revealing it through the funnel or on separate pages.

More on the rule of one page, one purpose
go.mattish.com/ecom10

THE LONGER YOU MAKE IT THE MORE YOU RISK THE USER SWITCHING OFF

MAILING LIST SIGN-UP

When was the last time you visited a new website and were immediately hit by a pop-up promoting their mailing list? Probably very recently. And when was the last time you thought "Great, a mailing list! Can't wait to sign up"? Probably a lot less recently.

Make sure you don't do something you wouldn't use on other sites. I understand the temptation to get users' email addresses as soon as possible. It can be expensive to acquire users so there's pressure to capture as many as you can to market to them again over email. However there are things to think about before blitzing the user with pop-ups and sign-up fields.

Have you given users enough time to look at your site? If you're popping up the message as soon as they land, the chances are they don't know much about what you offer yet and will immediately dismiss it.

Are you offering something of value? Requesting an email address requires offering something in return. In my experience, cash discounts or percentage discounts greater than 10% tend to get noticed. Something generic like 'updates and latest offers' doesn't.

You may be getting lots of user email addresses via your pop-ups but will these users ever open your emails? Increasingly users have specific spam email addresses for signing up to offers. You'll find plenty of articles on the web about sites who have increased sign-up rates with pop-ups, but very few will tell you whether those users then converted.

A deeper look at whether to use email pop-ups and how to best do it
go.mattish.com/ecom11

SIGN UP

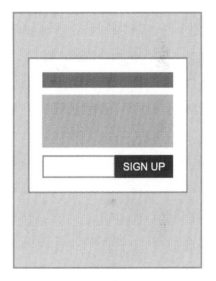

SIGN UP

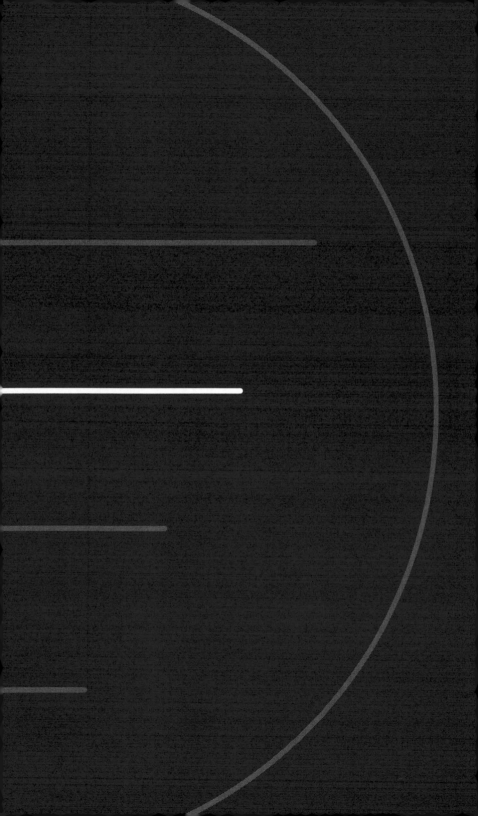

LISTINGS

The listings page is where users come to look through the products you have for sale. These pages are sometimes referred to as category pages, as this is where products are displayed by category, or search pages when users have entered specific search terms. Despite the possibility for different names they look very similar and mainly display a list of products.

If you've taken your users from your landing pages to this point then they should understand who you are and should be interested in what you're selling. Now they want to see the actual options for meeting their needs in your product range. This usually means sifting through lots of options with the help of a set of filters to narrow things down.

They will use this page to get a sense of the products you sell by judging them en masse—for example the range of prices available. They will also look at products individually to understand how they differ from each other.

REQUIREMENTS

The core things you need for almost all products are name, price, images, and an indication of product variations (like size and colour). You may need more than this if your product is more complex but each product should be presented consistently so it is easy to scan down the page and find information.

What other elements you require on your listings page will depend on what you're selling and your audience. Consider what information is needed to give users enough detail to differentiate and choose a product.

Are you selling something that is expensive, featuring locations or impressive detail? Then photography will be an important part of your offering. Are you selling something more functional like cleaning products or computer parts? In this case what the product looks like matters less compared to how it performs, making it a more rational purchasing decision, so focussing on product data makes more sense.

This stage of the funnel is about helping users find the right product, and as humans we're limited in how much information we can store in our head at any one time. If your site is small (with around 10-20 products) then you may not need filters and search fields, but they become more important the bigger a website gets. The more products you have, the more filters you will need to help people whittle things down.

SUCCESS

A listings page is successful if it moves users onto the product page, so this is your core conversion rate to watch. There's a bit more nuance to this as you want users to go to a product they might actually buy. This can be a fiddly thing to understand but a high number of listings page views per session in your web analytics could be a clue to look at this further.

If the user is viewing the listings page a lot it might be because they keep going to products that aren't right for them and then returning to listings. This suggests the listings aren't explaining product differences very well. This might be backed up by a lower time on page for products compared to listings, which isn't what you'd normally expect.

To find out the truth you'll need to dig into more qualitative data to see how users are actually behaving on the page. Research such as visitor recordings and user testing will help you with this. It's always a good idea to get a sense of how your users think and what motivates them towards making purchases.

These guidelines will break down all of the elements you could have on the page and how you can use them: get that balance right between images and information and you'll have a truly useful listings experience.

FILTERS - DESKTOP

Once you have more than about 30 products on your site you're going to need filters to help users find what they want. Users certainly don't want to waste time manually sifting through hundreds or thousands of products.

On desktop screens the best place for filters to live is the left hand side of the page—80% of the world's biggest ecommerce websites do this. Vertical filters on the left side are a well-understood pattern and make it easy for users to see their options alongside the results, whereas horizontal filter bars are often missed as users scroll.

Make it as easy as possible for users to apply these filters and turn them off. When they select an individual filter the results set should immediately update, so they can see that the changes are taking effect.

I'd recommend keeping your filter categories to a number that can comfortably fit on screen, to save users from needing to load more in. If you have filter categories with lots of values (brand name is a good example), it's best to show the most popular ones by default and then allow users to expand the list to see all of them.

Analysis of what 50 of the world's biggest ecommerce websites do with filters **go.mattish.com/ecom12**

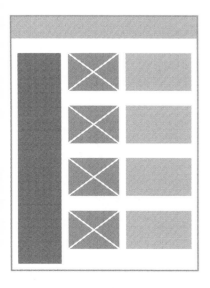

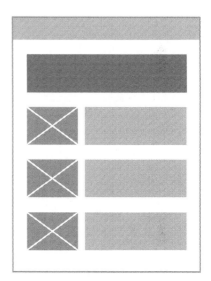

FILTERS - MOBILE

The vast majority of ecommerce sites (about 90% of those I've studied) have their filters in a pop-up or panel on mobile screen sizes. This makes sense when there isn't much space available but it does mean users aren't very likely to actually use them.

As a rule most users don't change defaults and this applies to opening a filters menu to select specific options. It's something that has been borne out in the ecommerce user tests I've watched. Thus finding products on listings pages is one area where the ecommerce browsing experience is superior on desktop.

Helping your users to filter means they're more likely to find a product that they actually want. The challenge for mobile is finding space-saving ways of doing so. One great method is to show just the most relevant filter category on the page with buttons showing the filter values. Tapping a value would load listings with that filter applied, at which point the next most relevant filter would show.

At the very least make sure your button to reach the full filter menu is obvious. It should also clearly indicate when a filter is applied, so users know when they are seeing a limited set of products.

Research into how 95% of users don't touch default settings
go.mattish.com/ecom13

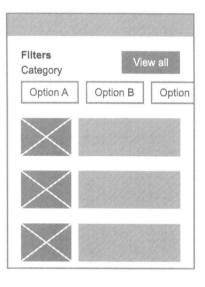

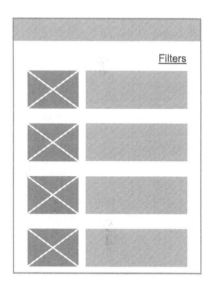

SEARCH FIELDS

A lot of ecommerce sites have a search field. It's a very useful thing when you have a lot of products, as it helps save users from browsing through several pages to find something they already know they want. But it's not enough just to chuck a search field in the header and be done with it. It can work a lot harder.

The biggest danger with free text search is that once you have a search field people can type pretty much anything in there (and they will). This can result in zero results screens, which are a frustrating experience for the user. To prevent this your search field must incorporate auto-complete and auto-suggest.

Auto-complete is when the field shows search terms that could be formed from the letters the user has started to type. This is particularly useful when you sell a limited set of things and you need to guide users to the right search terms.

Auto-suggest is when the field gives the user similar searches to the terms they have entered, or searches that are popular with other users of the site. You can also suggest individual products in order to take the user straight to those product pages and speed up the process. Between these options you can both guide the user away from dead-end searches and help educate them about the kind of products you sell.

📖 A lot more detail on effective auto-complete and auto-suggest fields
go.mattish.com/ecom14

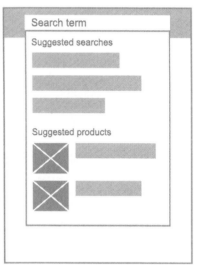

Search term

Suggested searches

Suggested products

Search term

DO YOU NEED A PRODUCT FINDER?

It's possible that a traditional search and listings model isn't the best approach for your site. Do you sell niche products? Does the user have to buy exactly the right thing or it won't be compatible with their needs? If the user needs guidance to reach the right outcome rather than just choosing something they like, then you might need a product finder.

A finder would usually exist in addition to search, although in some cases it could replace it altogether. The idea is that it helps guide the user step-by-step through the buying process. It asks users questions about their requirements, getting them to make a simple decision at each step, before presenting them with results that match their exact requirements.

For example on a site that sells beauty products the finder might ask users questions about their skin tone, face shape, and eye colour, in order to recommend the right makeup.

This is a great way to show expertise and gain trust from users, especially if it's an item that they don't buy very often, or if they just feel uncertain when shopping in your category. It could be something to implement if you are seeing a lot of products being returned because users are ordering the wrong size, product type, or wrong item altogether.

Some rules for designing good product finders
go.mattish.com/ecom15

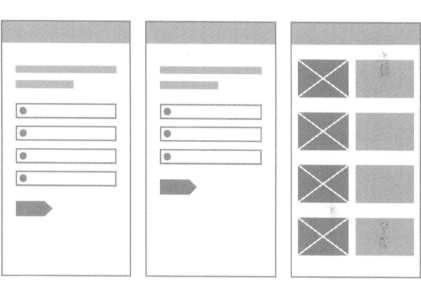

1 2 3

CATEGORY DESCRIPTIONS

It's always a good idea to supply the title of the product category at the top of a listings page, but plenty of sites have a whole header section displaying the title, a description, and a banner image. This can take up a chunk of space at the top of the page so you might wonder if it is necessary.

The full banner treatment is only really useful when you're selling niche products. A page listing 'chairs' doesn't need an explanation—this term is widely understood. A page listing 'osteopath ergonomic chairs' would be helped by having one, so all users understand what it is.

If you're selling something really specific, like a certain brand that very few other people sell there might be lots of features and benefits to explain. Don't do this on the category page itself as this is a place to view and compare products but instead link off to an information page (see page 166), where you can explain it fully. On that page should be a CTA to get back to the shop.

Another option is to put category descriptions at the bottom of the page. This is something a lot of sites do to get the SEO benefit without cluttering the design. Just remember that most users will miss any useful information contained within here.

Advice on writing search engine optimised category descriptions
go.mattish.com/ecom16

THE FULL EXPLANATION HELPS TO SELL NICHE PRODUCTS

MAPS

If you're selling something with a location—like holiday accommodation or venues—then a map is going to be a vital part of your listings page. Most users will be helped by knowing where places are when they make their choice.

Simply providing a map with every result on it will just overwhelm the user with too many options and can be hard to make sense of. Here are some things to think through in order to create a great map experience:

— What zoom level will you set the map to initially? Ideally you want it at a level that shows a manageable number of results (about 10) but this density is likely to vary by location so it may need to change.

— How much do you want the user to be able to zoom in/ out? Does it make sense for them to zoom all the way into the map or all the way out to continent-level? You'll probably want to limit this functionality.

— Can you group the results? One way to deal with lots of results is to group them into areas, creating a larger icon showing the number of results in that area. This makes sense if you have lots of results but only if the area groupings (such as districts in cities) are understood by users.

— Are you going to limit the number of results on screen? Another way to solve having lots of results is only to show a handful at once. If you do this then it needs to be clear to the user that more results are available by moving the map or changing search parameters.

More on this advice for maps with some real examples
go.mattish.com/ecom17

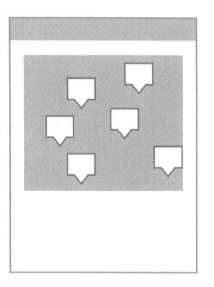

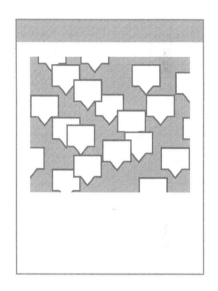

NAMES

Your products need names but there are many ways you can go about it. You could keep them very simple and stripped back ('The Z Hat') or you could be really funky and specific ('Wild Exotic Tropical Green Mush Scrub'). Is there really a right or wrong way? In my experience there are a few rules that make for strong and memorable names:

— Keep them fairly short (ideally no more than three words) or people will struggle to recall it.

— Make them unique—really generic titles are going to make it hard for the user to find it again ('classic t-shirt' in a site with 100s of t-shirts for example). Instead add a bit of personality with a name you won't find repeated elsewhere.

— If they're going to be very different, like the Swedish IKEA product names, then help users by displaying the product type next to it, e.g. 'Ektorp | Armchair'.

— Don't cram the titles with SEO information or product details, as much as marketing folk might want you to do this. Things like size and colour should be found in their relevant place on the page for comparison, and users shouldn't need to hunt for them within the title. It makes comparison hard.

The above rules are often broken if you're selling on a marketplace like Amazon where the title is the main place to get across the details of your product, so keyword-packing helps it appear in searches.

Recommendations for all product listing content, including titles
go.mattish.com/ecom18

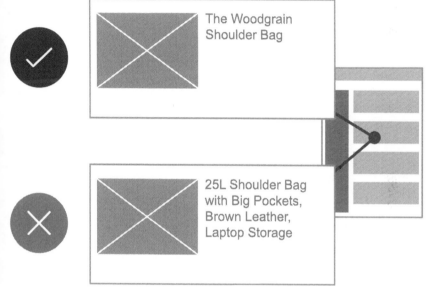

The Woodgrain
Shoulder Bag

25L Shoulder Bag
with Big Pockets,
Brown Leather,
Laptop Storage

DO YOUR USERS UNDERSTAND YOUR PRODUCT NAMES?

Product names alter perceptions. Very few ecommerce sites have such strong brands that users will be willing to learn a new language to understand what you're trying to sell. I've worked on a few ecommerce sites where the names didn't mean anything to the users and in user tests people completely ignored content that would have been right for them because they didn't want to risk clicking on something that they didn't understand.

This advice applies to including all sorts of things in your titles, from unclear terms, famous people, historic events, or specific location names. In particular be careful with names that people might struggle to pronounce, as it can cause them to miss the intended meaning altogether.

In addition, ambiguous wording means the user has to fill in the blanks and unless you've put a lot of effort into marketing your uniquely named things, it can mean they interpret things incorrectly.

For example I'd suggest erring on the side of calling an arty tourist trip in Paris aimed at an English-speaking audiences, The Great Art Of Paris, rather than something like Les Vieux Maitres de Paris. This is obviously clearer for tourists who don't speak the language and for lay people who may not even understand the meaning of the term 'Old Masters' in English.

Advice for testing out new product names
go.mattish.com/ecom19

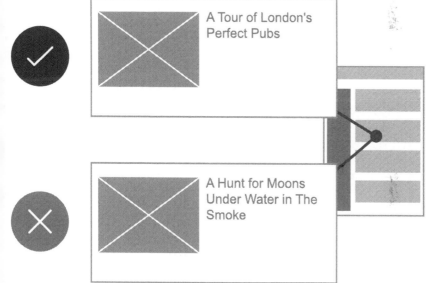

A Tour of London's Perfect Pubs

A Hunt for Moons Under Water in The Smoke

PRICES

Clearly the price should be present on your listings, as it's a vital piece of information. It's a huge driver of what people choose to look at, and being able to sort and filter by price is highly useful to users.

The most important thing is to make sure the price you display refers to the same thing on each product. For example, on a travel site all prices should either be the total price or the price per night. Mixing the two will only lead to confusion.

You should avoid the use of 'from' prices where possible as it doesn't give the user much to go on (just how high could costs go above that 'from' price?). This may require forcing the user to enter more information such as their dates of travel in order to generate an accurate price.

The price doesn't need to dominate the listing, as long as it's clearly stated users will spot it. But it's always worth designing with promotions and discounts in mind: these are likely to be more visually dominant and there needs to be space to show both the previous and the sale price.

Useful info on the psychology behind product pricing
go.mattish.com/ecom20

PRICE *IS A* HUGE *DRIVER OF* WHAT *PEOPLE* CHOOSE *TO* LOOK *AT*

THUMBNAIL IMAGES

Most ecommerce site listings pages show several products on screen at once. As a result the product images on listings (traditionally known as thumbnail images) have tended to be quite small, which can lead you to think that imagery isn't important here.

I'd recommend against falling into the default of using small thumbnail images. The image is a key part of helping the user make a decision about which product to select and in many cases it tells you a lot more than any text can. Things like clothing, furniture, and properties, all rely on the user being able to make a subjective distinction between the different things on offer.

I've worked on sites where the images haven't just been seen as a small visual indicator but a large part of the listing. Users always react very positively to this (it doesn't matter where they are on the site, good photography is always loved).

It can be hard to summarise some products in a single image, particularly experiential ones or locations. If you think something can be better sold in a few images then do so. Travel sites often have multiple photos in their thumbnails with a subtle arrow to scroll through them. Many clothing sites offer the option of showing the product on its own and being worn by a model.

Research into what top ecommerce sites do with their listings page images **go.mattish.com/ecom21**

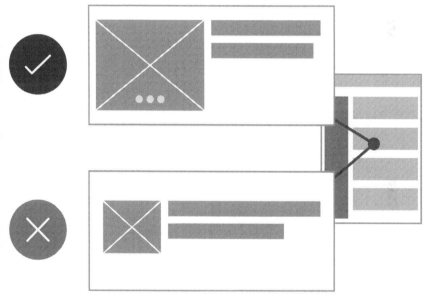

RATINGS

When ecommerce sites capture reviews, they almost always record a star rating for each product too. When should you show that to your users on the listings page?

They can be useful for many products, particularly if you are selling things that people don't buy very often or are technical in nature. For example, most people only buy a television every 5-10 years and are unlikely to be up to speed with technical jargon that could help them choose a product. User ratings thus become a very useful way of sifting through the many options to find the good stuff. Experiences that users may only do once, like visit a hotel or restaurant, also require other people's experiences to help them make a decision (hence the importance of TripAdvisor).

If you are selling luxury products that position themselves on quality and uniqueness, then ratings don't make so much sense. The nature of the brand tells users that the products are all of a high quality and aren't for comparing with other generic things.

When you show a rating there are two things it must include. The first is the maximum possible score, either visually (often via five stars) or in words. The second is how many people have rated the product in total to show how meaningful that score is, e.g. 200 people giving a score of 4.5 is more powerful than just two people giving a score of five.

Details on sorting by average rating weighted by number of ratings
go.mattish.com/ecom22

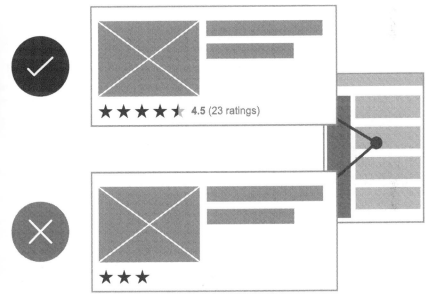

4.5 (23 ratings)

VARIATIONS

There are two ways to show if a product comes in variations of things like different colours/materials/ sizes. The first is to indicate with icons or text on the product listing. This gets confusing if you have a product with lots of variations, as users could miss all the configurations available to them.

The second is to make every option into a separate product that appears in the results. The danger here is that you flood your listings with similar-looking items. I've watched user tests where this is the case and it just confuses users, as they think they're seeing repetitions.

What's the right answer? Generally I'd go for having one product with an indicator of any variations. I follow these two rules of thumb when deciding if it's worth using separate products:

— Create a separate product if a variation means the price is radically different. This ensures you are appealing to users in an appropriate price bracket and don't shock them when they select a product variation that causes the price to double.

— Create a separate product if the size changes the use case of the product being sold. A change in size of suitcase could change its suitability from weekend breaks to two-week holidays. A change in length of surfboard would appeal to a different style of rider.

How selecting a colour should update the listing image too
go.mattish.com/ecom23

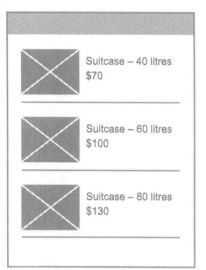

	Suitcase – 40 litres $70
	Suitcase – 60 litres $100
	Suitcase – 80 litres $130

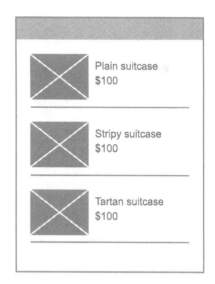

	Plain suitcase $100
	Stripy suitcase $100
	Tartan suitcase $100

SHOULD YOU USE 'ADD TO BASKET' LINKS?

One aspect of a listings page you'll find on some websites and not others, is a button to add a product to your basket. It's easy to think that every website should have this—after all, what's better than getting more products into the basket? Well, it depends on what you sell.

There are couple of questions I ask to determine whether the listings should have this button: 1. Are the products you sell something users buy often? 2. Do users tend to order several different products at once? If the answer to these is yes, then your site should benefit from an 'add to basket' button on listings.

For example, on a supermarket website where the user shops regularly and knows what type of cereal they like, being able to quickly add to the basket will be a huge help. The hassle of going into a product page each time would slow the journey down hugely.

Compare this to a user on specialist clothing site looking to buy an expensive winter coat. They're going to want to get the decision right, and will certainly be checking the product page to see the details. They're very unlikely to immediately click 'add to basket' from listings so it would be taking up space unnecessarily.

A thread on whether this button helps conversions
go.mattish.com/ecom24

DO YOUR USERS ORDER SEVERAL DIFFERENT PRODUCTS AT ONCE?

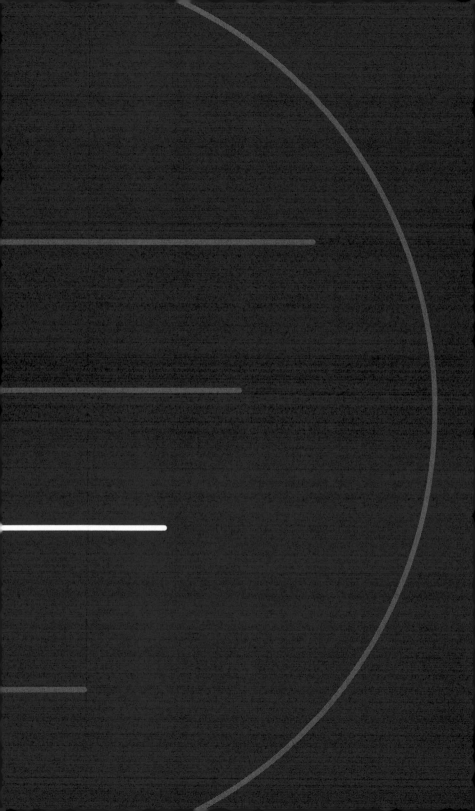

PRODUCT

The product page is where all the details about an individual product live. It doesn't matter whether your ecommerce site sells physical items or experiences, they can be considered products as long as they have attributes to be shown and described. The product page performs a similar role to packaging where the customer can't see or touch the actual item but still wants to understand both the specifications and what it looks like.

I would argue that this is the most important step in the ecommerce funnel, because it has to convince users to buy. It's probably where the user will spend most of their time considering the purchase. A good product page can also be found directly via social media, email, or by getting to the top of Google search results.

REQUIREMENTS

When shopping, whether consciously or not, the user will cycle through three different modes of thought before making a purchase, and the product page must solve for each of them. I categorise these modes as dreams, realities, and fears. Not all products require the user to consider all three but the more expensive and complex the product, the more all of them will be needed.

DREAMS

The dreams phase is the first stage and it is where the user needs to feel excited about what is being offered. You should appeal to their senses and get the user to *want* to buy the product. Without this they won't make the effort to dig into the details of the item.

Ideally the user should see themselves owning or experiencing the product and the benefits it will bring them.

elements that promote this should appear obviously on the page (often near the top). This is typically done through the likes of high resolution photos, videos of products in action, or carefully written descriptions.

This stage may not apply much to practical or technical items (e.g. cleaning products, DIY materials) but for almost everything else it is important. Done well, this will elevate your site above others selling similar products.

REALITIES

The details section follows the user's excitement about the product on offer and helps get them into thinking about the practicalities of making the purchase. The user now starts to get rational and consider whether the item meets their needs.

Things like feature lists and specifications will help the user reach a decision. It could be clothing coming in the right fit; food being ethically sourced; hotels having a pool or gym; or a car having the right colour options. Every product requires this kind of information or it is incomplete.

For all products the most important of these realities is whether it comes in at the right price. This is where most of the contemplating takes place and will determine whether this item is the right choice for the user.

FEARS

This is about allaying the users' fears and it is more important the more money a user is spending. This is where they need to be reassured that the product does what it claims and that the website isn't exaggerating.

The website can provide a lot of information here but it's also helpful for a user to consult others' experiences. As well as things like FAQs, shipping information, and returns or cancellation policies, you can assist by displaying customer reviews and ratings for the product. All products require some level of information here but it particularly matters the first time a user purchases from a site.

SUCCESS

The ultimate success metric is whether users click that 'buy now' or 'add to basket' button. For expensive products you should see your page as a source of leads (where users go on to purchase later) as much as instant purchases.

This page must work for users who are immediately ready to buy as well as those who want to study every detail before making a purchase (any store will get a mix of these users). It is by organising your information into clear sections you can allow the confident buyers to scan quickly through, or the more meticulous to dig into the details.

The following advice will help you with the most common elements, but remember the product page is also a chance to show some personality. It's where the product comes to life, so it can be less formulaic than functional pages like listings and checkout.

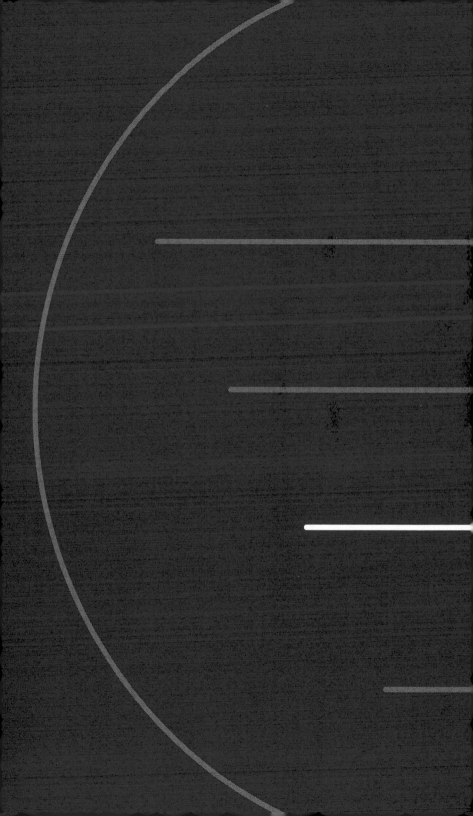

IMAGES

There's a big hurdle at the heart of selling online. Users can't see the product in real life or reach out and touch it (at least not yet anyway), so how are they going to decide which is right for them?

Imagery is hugely important in ecommerce, but it is most vital on the product page, so it's odd when websites demote their imagery here. Don't be one of those websites that has photos but makes them frustratingly small — put them front and centre.

I've lost count of the number of user tests I've watched where the thing users have got most excited about is looking through product photos. Users are often keen to spend the most time studying them to really understand what they're buying.

To look professional, your imagery should feature consistently styled photography, taken with good lighting. Don't fall for convenience and just put up the first pictures you can get: poorly lit camera phone pics won't cut it.

If you're selling experiences or something less physical, imagery can still be important to show the benefits of the service. For example when selling cheese tasting, the product isn't lumps of cheese but people gathered together, learning and having a good time.

📖 A guide to creating great ecommerce product images
go.mattish.com/ecom25

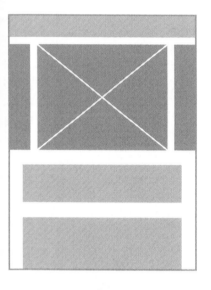

BUY BUTTON

There are several potential actions you can have on a product page that require buttons: check stock, choose size, enquire, live chat, check availability, add to wish list. These can all be useful but should any of them be top priority?

No. There should only be one button standing out amongst the rest: the button to buy the product, or add it to the basket. If you've got the user interested in a product, they shouldn't have to guess at how to give you their money. This page has one primary goal so help the user reach it.

Your button should use a colour only used for primary actions. Don't blend it in, don't make the wording unclear, don't prioritise other actions on the page. Also if you make it clear and unmissable it doesn't need to follow the user around the page on a sticky nav (see page 106).

Avoid ever greying out this button as users are likely to think they can't buy the item. Even if you need a size to be selected before they can buy, let users click the button before opening the size menu with an explanatory error message. When something actually is out of stock or unavailable, you could replace it with a link to a contact form so they can ask to be informed when it is available again.

A comprehensive guide to designing strong buttons
go.mattish.com/ecom26

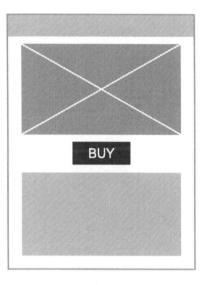

ALTERNATIVES TO BUYING

There's a problem in the ecommerce funnel model we've been following. It's great for pushing users towards purchasing products but if they've found something that they aren't ready to buy yet, the page can become a dead end.

An ecommerce product page with a buy button as the *only* action just gives the user a binary choice between buying now or leaving altogether and the theory of 'single option aversion' states they're more likely to do the latter. It also fails to help those who aren't quite ready to buy for whatever reason. The solution is a subtler secondary action, which doesn't compete with your primary one.

A good secondary option is an enquiry form. This way if the user is uncertain about buying or has further questions, you give them a place where they can ask for help. This enquiry could then lead to a conversion over email/phone or at a later date.

If you have bricks and mortar shops, then another handy option here is a 'find in store' button. This could direct users to a nearby store or check stock levels, for those who want to see the product in-person before buying.

If you have a phone number, put this near the buy button too. It's helpful for those users who are in a rush and need instant help, and not the extra work of a form.

The concept of 'single option aversion' explained
go.mattish.com/ecom27

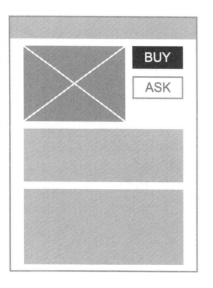

PRICE

The price is the price, right? In some product categories there can only be one price, but there are actually many ways you can value things. If you aren't completely clear about how your pricing works, users will end up confused.

This is a particular problem when selling experiences and holidays, which have variable prices and users will come with their own expectations of how things should be priced depending on the size of the group they are used to booking for.

I've watched user tests of a holiday site where they just displayed a single 'from' price. This was a bad idea: some users thought this referred to a total, some thought a price per person, and some a price per day. The website even put a price 'per guest per day' underneath the main price to show how good value it was. Combining this with their previous assumptions led some users to think the big total was a flat rate and the smaller amount below was an *additional* cost per guest per day. A minefield.

If there's room for ambiguity then users will get confused, which could cost you trust and sales. When selling anything that isn't a single price, take the space to make sure you carefully describe what these prices mean—at this stage of the journey the user won't want you to be vague.

Advice on where to put your prices on the page
go.mattish.com/ecom28

BUY

ASK

$950 trip price
+ $150 per extra person
+ $400 room upgrade
+ $50 arrival drinks

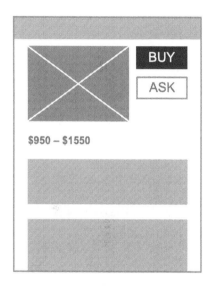

BUY

ASK

$950 – $1550

VARIANT OPTIONS

As covered in the listings section (see page 66),
it's common for products to be offered in variations.
This can be colour, size, flavour, or something else.
The product page is where users ultimately make
that choice. To help them you should avoid dumping
these options in dropdown menus.

They need to sit above the 'add to basket' button to show
users that they need selecting first. Where possible they
should be visual buttons to help the user see all the choices
and they should make clear when a variation means a
change in price. If the variant changes the look of the
product (such as the colour) then selecting it should update
the main product image, so it leaves no doubt as to what will
be ordered.

When it comes to size selection it's best not to have a default
size, otherwise you could easily end up with users adding the
preset size rather than they one they want. This could lead
to lots of returns and frustrated customers. The exception
is when you already have this information from a user's
preferences (see page 156).

Details on how to display product variations
go.mattish.com/ecom29

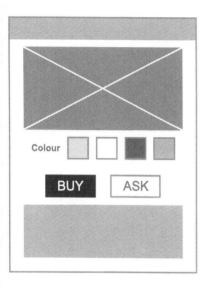

Colour

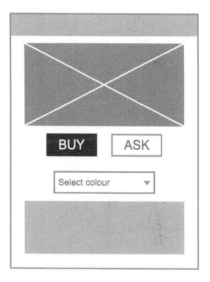

BUY   ASK

Select colour   ▼

DETACILS

A common repeated behaviour we know from years
of usability research is that users don't read when
browsing. Instead they quickly scan and jump around.
Despite this, I'm going to say that you can include
a lot of text on your product pages.

Why? Great copy is an undervalued tool in ecommerce
websites. It's a chance to explain the details of a product and
set it apart from the competition. Not all users will want to
read it but there will be many who need further convincing
and reassuring before they're happy to part with their money.

However it should be highly scannable—don't just present
it to the user in a single block but break it up into relevant
sections. Design it so that users can get the key information
at first viewing and more information if they need. You should
utilise sub-headings, bullet points, tabs, expandable sections,
and tables, to make the details easier to consume and help
people find the bit they want.

Examples of details you might need are descriptions, size
guides, shipping details, dimensions, features, performance
statistics, and FAQs. A lot of this can be repeated across
product pages as it stays the same but it is always useful for
the user to have it to hand, rather than needing to click a link.

Advice for making those product descriptions compelling
go.mattish.com/ecom30

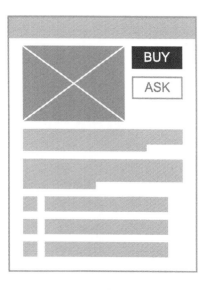

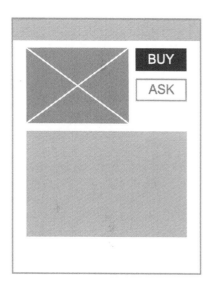

PRODUCT VIDEO

I touched on video in the landing page chapter (see page 34), where it works best as a background scene-setting feature. On the product page you can make the video a bit more detailed and something for users to engage with.

Even just a short clip of video can get across a lot more information than the best photo, especially for products where scale and fit are particularly important to understand and human interaction adds context. Videos are useful for niche products, especially those that are complex and require some explaining to users.

If you want your video to actually get watched then don't hide it in a gallery of images (many sites make it the last one where a lot of users will miss it), but instead have it be visible on the page. Another great way to make sure people watch it is to keep it under a minute long and tell people this, so they know there's no big commitment when clicking play.

📖 Examples of videos working both for product explanation and marketing **go.mattish.com/ecom31**

USP

The importance of explaining your brand's USP was covered on the landing page (see page 20). Whilst you may think you've already told people, here is a good place to bring it up again.

For starters it's possible users have missed it at other points on your site and may have just landed here. In addition, as the user is getting close to buying you'll want to remind them why they should buy this product from you, rather than something similar from somewhere else. The message can be told through copy or more creatively with photography, video, or infographics.

It's a chance to relate your USP to individual products too. I've seen some great clothing sites that make their differentiator the provenance of the garments and that they know exactly where the materials have come from. They introduce the concept on the landing page but follow this through by displaying the exact sources for each product's materials on their respective pages.

📖 A guide showing ecommerce sites that get their USP across well
go.mattish.com/ecom32

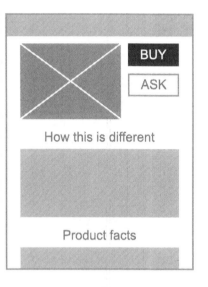

How this is different

Product facts

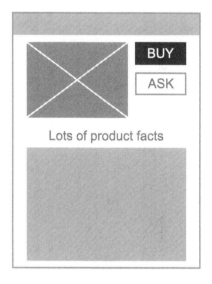

Lots of product facts

REVIEWS

We all know that people use reviews to make decisions about whether to buy many types of product. We've almost certainly all done it ourselves. In fact they're widely seen as a conversion improver.

This doesn't mean that you just dump all the text from your reviews onto your product pages. They can work harder than that.

You can make them more useful by splitting them into sections, for things like product quality, size feedback, shipping feedback, etc. This can be done by getting customers to answer a few short questions rather than just requesting a long review.

You can also gather information about your users and display this to help people identify relevant reviews to them. For example most holiday sites tell users the type of trip the reviewing guest was on (e.g. business or leisure) and their group type (e.g. couple or family). Equally I've seen DIY sites show users if the reviewer is a tradesman, which helps the user know the level of experience the review is based on.

How websites make their ratings and reviews more useful
go.mattish.com/ecom33

Reviews from people like you (5)

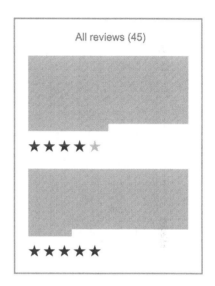

All reviews (45)

DO YOU NEED REVIEWS?

Whilst reviews are great, they aren't always possible for every site. For starters you need to have a decent number of customers to present reviews for every product. It can look worse just having one or two of them appearing on a few products.

In some cases reviews may not be a good fit for the brand— high fashion and luxury products tend not to present user reviews as they've worked to make the brand a guarantee of quality.

Even if you don't have reviews, you can still build trust with your users by replacing them with other methods of being candid and transparent. One option is to use social media to show how people are using the product. An Instagram feed of home-shot photos of your product in people's lives is a nice counterpoint to slick brand photography.

Another option is to use copy to write truthfully in a section away from the sales description. A few honest bullet points on things the user needs to know can work well. I worked on an accommodation site without reviews but with a section called 'home truths' that informed users about restrictions with the property, and proved very popular. This can also be solved with a short FAQs section, where you can tackle known questions and issues that previous customers have had.

📖 The reasons you may not want to use reviews and examples of alternatives **go.mattish.com/ecom34**

YOU CAN STILL BUILD TRUST BY BEING

CANDID

AND

TRANSPARENT

RELATED PRODUCTS

When you scroll to the bottom of a product page what do you find? In the vast majority of websites, it's a strip of images of other products, and a message telling you how you 'might be interested' in them. It's a last attempt to get you to keep browsing if you've reached the bottom of the page and haven't found what you wanted.

Amazon tends to have three or four if these strips per product page, so it's a good idea for you to have at least one right? Well, only if they're helpful to the user.

In a few years of working with one site, I discovered that the average click-through rate on related products was 0.3%. This is poor, especially considering the user is quite far down the funnel and interested at this point. A big part of the issue was they just weren't compelling enough.

It comes down to whether you are giving the user a reason to click/tap them. If you're going to have related products then you can't just state that they're 'similar'. It's important to make that relationship meaningful and useful. The strongest approach is to manually curate them, for example giving suggestions of other clothing that creates an outfit with the item being viewed.

A guide to getting more out of your related products
go.mattish.com/ecom35

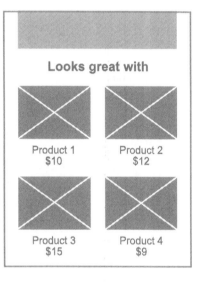

Looks great with

Product 1
$10

Product 2
$12

Product 3
$15

Product 4
$9

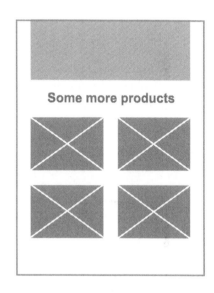

Some more products

CROSS-SELLING

Cross-selling or up-selling (or whatever you want to call offering more products) can be a powerful tool to boost sales. However you've got to do more than just throw products at users. You want to do it in such a way that it is helpful rather than seeming like a sales tactic.

If you're selling expensive products and the average order is one item then you can consider a whole page or pop-up to offer users relevant accessories. This could appear after they've added something to a basket and as they're likely to only see it once, users shouldn't find it a hassle.

If users are likely to be adding multiple things to their basket then an extra step after adding every product to the basket would quickly get frustrating. Instead make any offers that relate to individual products on the product page. When you have a general promotion that applies across all purchases then show it on the basket.

You might even consider putting a cross-sell after payment, as users have shown they trust you at this stage and you have all the information to immediately charge their card again. Once you have made the sale, it's a no-lose approach.

Examples of big brands using cross-sells in different places
go.mattish.com/ecom36

THIS CAN BE A POWERFUL TOOL TO BOOST SALES

SOCIAL BUTTONS

Facebook, Twitter, Pinterest, Instagram, LinkedIn, Snapchat. Your users probably hang out at one or more of these social networks. So should you give them sharing buttons for those services? Many ecommerce sites present those little icons in the hope that it will encourage people to promote their wares around the web. Unfortunately, they're almost certainly a waste of time.

No-one clicks them. Actually 0.2% of people do, according to one study. What's more, adding them to your site might seem like a tiny snippet of code but it comes with lots of extra stuff that slows your page speed down. It also introduces their tracking code which effectively spies on your users' behaviour. This should be no small consideration.

The average user doesn't want to go broadcasting for brands without something in it for them. At most they might want to share in private with a friend or family member, through email or an instant messaging service like WhatsApp. If you want to make it easy for users to share your content then consider giving users links that they can copy and paste and so put wherever they want.

A study showing how few people actually use sharing buttons on mobile **go.mattish.com/ecom37**

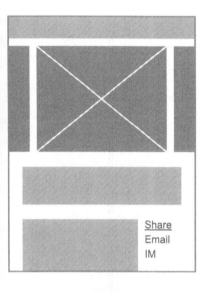

Share
Email
IM

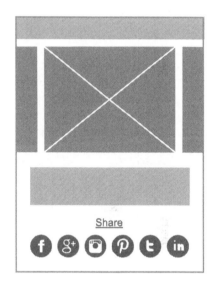

Share

ADDED TO BASKET

The patterns of ecommerce websites can feel so engrained in designers that they don't need to explain everything to the user. Everyone knows that when an item is added to the basket, the basket can be reached by clicking that icon (usually in the top right of the page). Don't they?

The vast majority or users probably do, but even if only one or two don't, why risk not explaining it? Once something is added, provide an overlay showing that the product is now in the basket with a link to get there. You can also supply a link for users to go straight to the checkout itself, to help speed along the buying process.

You can use this overlay to indicate the position of the basket in the navigation. This has the added benefit of giving users confirmation of their actions and an understanding what the site is doing (a key part of UX design). I recommend not automatically taking the user to the basket as this will get annoying if they have multiple products to purchase and need to navigate away from it each time.

📖 A few different ways the add to basket changes can be displayed
go.mattish.com/ecom38

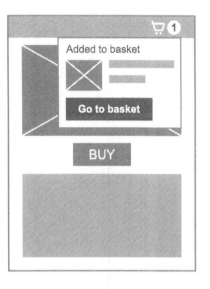

Added to basket

Go to basket

BUY

BUY

WHAT'S YOUR SPECIAL FEATURE?

We've established that there are a lot of standard elements your product page should have but is there specific information your site should have that others don't? There's often something, and it will be integral to the product itself and/or your USP.

You could present it via an animation, imagery, or a custom module. It could show how your product is assembled, show size and fit on clothing sites, or something much more bespoke that is added to the standard template.

Does your site offer only vegan ingredients in your products? Make sure people know with a section showing how those ingredients are the star, giving extra details on their provenance.

Is the most important thing about your product its compact size and what you can fit in there? Go a step above and show how the size compares to other small items to help it become more tangible in the user's mind.

Some examples of sites that have a special feature
go.mattish.com/ecom39

IS THERE *INFORMATION* YOUR *SITE* CAN *HAVE* THAT *OTHERS* DON'T?

STICKY NAVIGATION

Many product pages can end up being very long with all the details you have to tell users. Some websites will give the user a navigation that 'sticks' to the top or bottom of the screen when they scroll, with links to jump to sections of the page along with a 'buy' button. It seems sensible but in most cases this is overkill.

Most ecommerce sites now get the majority of their traffic from mobile devices (with the number only likely to rise). Sticky navigations take up a lot of screen real estate on already-small screens. One such site that I measured a sticky navigation at the top and bottom, reduced the available screen space by a huge 28%.

It's sites with long product pages and lots of detail that feel the need for sticky navigation. However these are typically for products where users take a long time to make a purchase. Pushing the 'buy now' button in front of them may not make a lot of difference to that lead time. Scrolling, on the other hand, is the easiest interaction on the web. As long as your 'buy' button is near the top of the page and clearly stands out, users will be able to find it.

One time it truly makes sense to have a sticky element on the page is when it is very long and the user can alter prices by selecting different options. In this case a sticky area keeping the user up to date with their running total can be highly useful, and is a prime place to include a CTA.

A weigh up of the pros and cons of a sticky navigation
go.mattish.com/ecom40

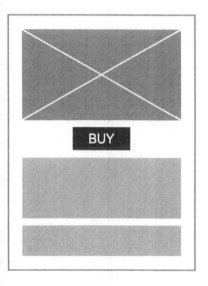

BUY

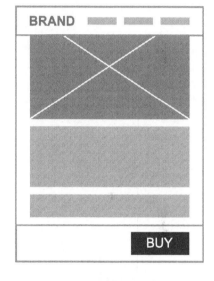

BRAND

BUY

CHECKOUT

The checkout flow is the sharp end of the ecommerce funnel: if the user has got this far then they have shown that they are very keen on what you're selling and are ready to make a purchase. The checkout is the functional step of getting the requisite information to make that happen.

It's often the most formulaic part of the site and as a result it is an area where you can find a lot of design advice. Despite this, plenty of mistakes still get made by companies: according to ecommerce specialists the Baymard Institute, 69% of users still abandon their baskets (combined from 40 studies, as of 2018).

Checkout flows are essentially about form-filling and users often find this dull. As a result they don't pay too much attention and are prone to making mistakes. Whatever you can do to make this easier or more convenient is valuable here.

REQUIREMENTS

There are really only four potential sections to a checkout flow. You may not need all of them but you shouldn't need any more than this. These four are the basket or product customisations; delivery information; billing information; and payment details. These steps could be separate pages or they could just be sections on a single page, as long as they are split out so it is clear for the user what is required at each point.

1A. BASKET

When a user can buy multiple products on your website at once then you'll require some kind of basket functionality to contain the products they want. The first tips in this chapter are specific to what you need in a basket, and a few others are possible candidates to put there.

1B. PRODUCT CUSTOMISATIONS

If you don't have a basket then you're likely to have a product customisation section, which tends to only exist on more complex services or experiences. Examples are seat selections for trains and planes or booking add-on services. These should come first in the checkout, as they are likely to relate to the product page that the user has just been looking at, so it naturally continues that journey. This way you ease the user into the checkout flow and get them to build their commitment to buying by making the product more personal.

2. DELIVERY INFORMATION

If you will be sending items to customers you'll require the user to choose which delivery service they want, an address to deliver to, and probably a phone number for delivery drivers to contact. It's important to show this near the start as it could alter the price and you want to allow users to see this early rather than spring it on them at the end. In addition if a user is keen to get something by a certain date they'll want to find out quickly if this is possible.

3. BILLING INFORMATION

Billing information is a step which is going to be required by almost all sites as it checks payment card details match the person paying. It is required by most payment providers, and usually means a name and address (you can speed up this step by asking the user if it's the same as the delivery one, which it often is). You should ask for an email address by this point so you can contact them about their order—and if it's a digital product, this will form the delivery mechanism.

DESIGNING ECOMMERCE WEBSITES

Finally we reach the payment details, which is a step every flow must have. Here users enter their all-important card details, or choose a payment wallet (sometimes this can be entered earlier to encompass other steps). This usually comes last in the flow because it involves a third party provider and you'll want to be sure you've collected everything you need first before sending users to them.

SUCCESS

The linear nature of a checkout flow means there's a clear metric as to whether something succeeds or not: either the user proceeds to the next step and ultimately pays or they don't. This makes it easy to monitor the data and see whether it is working. You should have a funnel measuring how successful these steps are and the one with the lowest conversion is your first port of call to improve.

It is often worth starting all of your website improvements here. It should be easier to get someone who has entered the checkout flow to convert, over someone who has just landed on your site.

With the convenience of payment wallets on mobile, the checkout flow is one step in the ecommerce funnel whose days may be numbered—certainly in the sense of having a custom one for every store. If you're going build a direct relationship with your customers, then your checkout will have to be super-smooth and easy to use to compete against the massive convenience of single-tap payments. The guides in this chapter should help you with that aim.

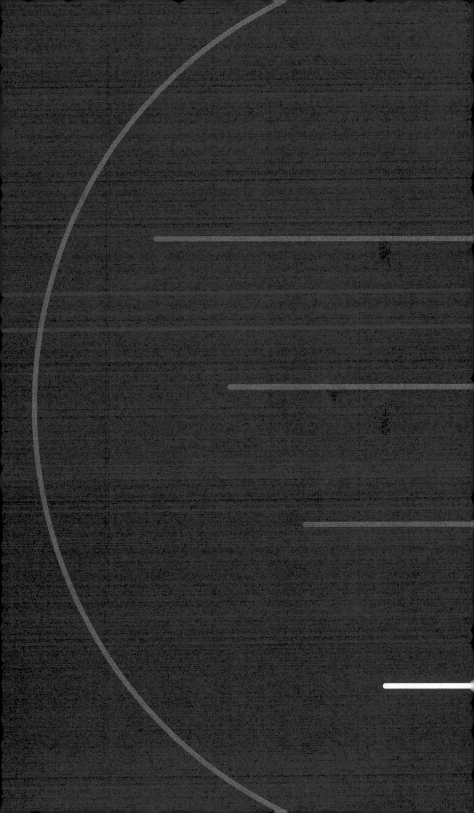

BASKET - PRODUCTS

Of course a basket should show users the products within it—that's what it's for! But just *how* should these products be displayed?

Some sites will skimp on the details thinking that the user already knows what they've put in there. However a key use of the basket is for double-checking and re-assurance that they've added the right thing. Some users may treat the basket as a running shortlist, adding a bunch of items before selecting the ones they actually want to buy.

As such the products in the basket are required to be similar to a listings page: they need to provide key information to the user and allow them to compare. Make sure you display the product title, a recognisable image (not too tiny), any variations such as size or colour, and of course the price. If you have space, allow users to edit their chosen variations here to save them having to go back to the product page.

Part of checking before paying will consist of making sure the right number of items have been ordered so allow users to change quantities here, including letting users remove items from their basket altogether. Ideally the user shouldn't have to click an 'update' button to apply their changes.

A deep dive into the different forms of quantity field you can use
go.mattish.com/ecom41

Your basket

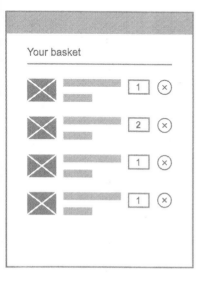

Your basket

BASKET - SHIPPING COST

Shipping and delivery charges are one of those things that users tend to hate. Free delivery is expected now: people can become quite irrational and a $5 charge can put them off making a $100 order. Unfortunately free is not always possible from the point of view of the seller, particularly where international shipping is concerned.

For a basket the simple rule is as follows: if the shipping cost will alter the total then the user needs to see it at this stage. If you ship internationally then get users to specify their country so they can see the cost. Of course if you don't ship internationally, you should state this here before users get too far along the checkout.

You're likely to have a few different delivery options but you only need to show the one (probably the cheapest) on the basket, though do make it clear how fast this delivery will be. It's also a good idea to show users how much they need to add to their basket to qualify for free shipping, as this can entice users to increase the order value.

How to display delivery charges, including non-standard ones
go.mattish.com/ecom42

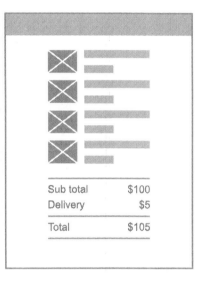

Sub total	$100
Delivery	$5
Total	$105

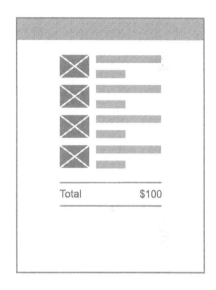

Total	$100

ACCEPTED PAYMENT METHODS

Is your site willing to take the more costly American Express, or the more obscure Discover card, or will it accept Android Pay? You might have a website that is popular in a country like China and users will want to know if it accepts WeChat Pay.

Showing the accepted payment methods is one of those default bits of site furniture that you can think users ignore. It matters because the number of payment methods are only on the increase. Whilst it's a given that a site will accept Visa and Mastercard, the other options are myriad and need stating.

Your list of logos doesn't need to take up a lot of space (and it certainly doesn't need to distract from getting people to payment) but it does need to be comprehensive. It's worth stating on the basket before users start filling in their checkout details. As sites grow they'll attract customers from new locations who need to know if they can pay the way they want.

A handy set of credit card logos to design with
go.mattish.com/ecom43

THE NUMBER OF PAYMENT METHODS ARE ONLY ON THE INCREASE

PROMO CODE FIELD

The best place to put the promo code field is the subject of a lot of debate in ecommerce circles. Most sites require one for allowing users to redeem offers and sometimes to run their voucher/credit note system, so not having one at all is rarely an option.

Plenty of articles will tell you that when a user sees a promo code field they will be inspired to go searching for a discount, which could risk them not returning to your site. Whilst it's hard to find research proving this, the sheer prevalence of voucher code websites and tools for finding discounts, show that people love to use them.

To play it safe it's best to keep the field fairly small or hidden by default. You want users who have a code and are looking for the field to be able to find it, but it not to interrupt people who haven't considered it.

It's also best to put the promo code field at the very start of the checkout process or in the basket itself. This is because you want users to see that they can use their discount. If it's hidden away on the payment step then some users will assume there isn't the option and will leave frustrated.

📖 The pros and cons of using voucher codes
go.mattish.com/ecom44

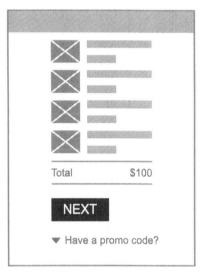

Total $100

NEXT

▼ Have a promo code?

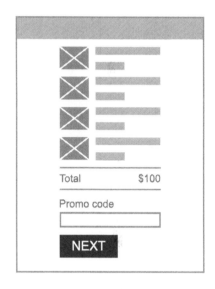

Total $100

Promo code

NEXT

CREDIBILITY MESSAGES

The basket and checkout is a place where users are likely to pause before making payment. At this point they will consider whether they want to buy now or maybe hold off for a bit. Any doubts they have will get magnified at this time. Credibility messages can help smooth the road here, and some common ones include:

— Badges showing that your checkout is secure;

— Scores showing that you are well reviewed (from sites like TrustPilot);

— Headings showing that there is a returns/refund policy.

All of these can be displayed in the footer without taking up huge amounts of space—you don't need to over-indulge in this practice. I've watched user tests where the site showed whole reviews or testimonials from customers and linked off to all sorts of extra information. It looked like too much work to understand and was promptly ignored by everyone.

Whilst users want to reassure themselves at a glance and check everything looks above-board, they're unlikely to want to do in-depth reading at this point.

⊞ This research found that adding pretty much any icon increases trust
go.mattish.com/ecom45

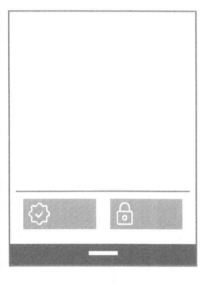

Reviews

GUEST CHECKOUT

This is an old and established piece of advice but worth repeating: allow users to go through checkout as a guest without making them sign up for an account. All sites should be doing this by now.

One of the biggest barriers to checkout completion is asking your users to sign up or create an account at the start. It adds that extra bit of hassle and thought to someone's journey: "Do I need to? Shall I just go to another site that I'm already registered with?". Asking for passwords is getting in the way, when at this point you should be getting out of the way and making it easy for them to part with their cash.

Even if you're a site where the user is likely to want to log back in later—like an accommodation or transport provider—you still don't have to get the user to create a password up front. You can get them to create it at the end of the process, when their order is placed (see page 146).

Be smart about it: the user didn't come to register for your site, they came to buy your product or service. Make the sale before asking for more.

Research showing 37% of users exit when asked up front to make an account **go.mattish.com/ecom46**

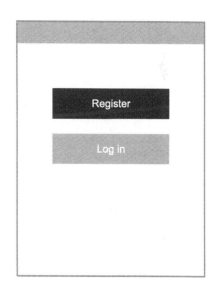

WALLETS

Payment wallet services such as PayPal, Apple Pay and Android Pay are on the rise. It's increasingly common to see them as options on ecommerce checkout flows. In fact they may kill off the standard checkout altogether.

Perhaps you might see them as a threat to gathering your users' information but they represent a new reality. Entering a password, fingerprint, or face scan and then being able to immediately complete checkout is so much more convenient than filling out forms. With ecommerce being dominated by mobile, easy payment is essential.

The benefits should outweigh any negatives. The sheer ease of use should encourage more users to complete checkout with you. There's also a security benefit as users will likely feel safer with a wallet as intermediary if they haven't heard of your brand before. Across the user tests I've run on checkout flows, I regularly hear comments like "I much prefer the option of using PayPal" and "I'm very security conscious and will only pay using PayPal".

📖 How wallets are replacing cash and cards in India (a massive mobile market) **go.mattish.com/ecom47**

THEY MAY

KILL OFF

THE STANDARD ECOMMERCE CHECKOUT

ALTOGETHER

CHECKOUT NAVIGATION

When first creating an ecommerce website it can be tempting to just have the standard website navigation on the checkout flow. You should resist doing this. Pretty much all the site-wide links should be removed from checkout pages.

This is a key point in the journey where users have expressed a strong interest in buying, so make it as easy as possible for them to do that. If they suddenly spot a new type of product in the navigation they may click it, read about it, compare it to one on another site, and forget to convert with you.

Take a look at any major brand's checkout page. The design will be a stripped back version of the main site, often with just a logo (which may or may not link to the homepage) in the header and only terms and conditions links in the footer. If they need extra information about something then provide it in-situ with tooltips and pop-ups that don't take them away.

The only links you should add in are ones between steps in a multi-page checkout. Showing the steps in the flow is also helpful to give users a rough guide to the length of the process. The process should feel more manageable this way and the user gets the reward of a mini-goal when they complete each one.

📖 This older theory behind enclosing the checkout is still valid
go.mattish.com/ecom48

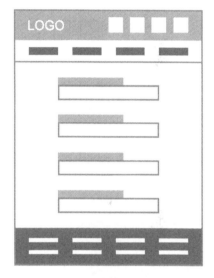

LAYOUT

It's common to want to fit lots in a small space on checkout pages. Perhaps you think that by using two (or even three) columns you can fit more above the fold and help the user to fill out their information quickly. This would be a mistake: more than one column will only make your checkout harder to complete.

You should stack all fields vertically (including things like first and last name). A checkout page naturally has a vertical flow from top to bottom. When you add columns you create an extra dimension and now the user has to work out when to look across and when to go down. I've watched many user tests of checkout flows with extra columns and users inevitably miss fields, cause errors, and have to go back to find them.

A single direction of focus helps the form itself act as a progress bar, as the user is able to see what they have and haven't filled in, and where they're up to on the page. The best approach is to design your checkout for mobile first, as with mobile you're unlikely to have the space for an anything other than one column anyway. You can then centre that layout on tablet and desktop (maybe with slightly wider fields).

A study showing users complete single column forms quicker than multi-column forms **go.mattish.com/ecom49**

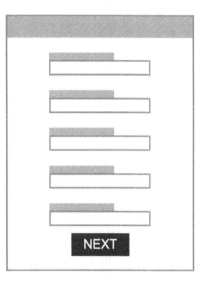

NEXT

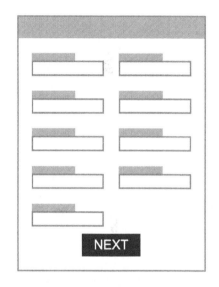

NEXT

ORDER SUMMARY

There's one exception to when checkout content can live outside of a single column layout and that's if it's non-interactive. It can contain information that won't matter if a user misses it.

A good example which should be present on all checkout flows is a summary of the user's basket. Even if you don't have a separate basket page on your website, you should show users what they are ordering throughout the checkout. Not only is it helpful if they need to check something, it also reassures users that they're paying for the right things. Making a payment can be an intimidating moment, particularly if it's for a large amount.

Despite its usefulness, it is ultimately secondary information and so can sit in an expandable section on mobile or can be positioned on the right side on desktop. The section itself can look a lot like a basket (see page 114) but as the checkout should be closed off from the rest of the site, you don't need to link to the product pages. Otherwise images, titles, variants, and price are all useful to maintain.

A look at how big ecommerce sites show order summaries on mobile **go.mattish.com/ecom50**

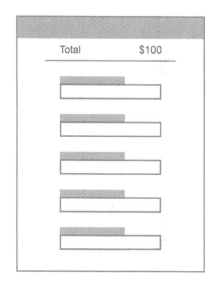

DELIVERY INFORMATION

If you are mailing products to your users then there are two essential pieces of delivery information you should supply for each option, and an extra one that can be useful. In research I carried out, when users saw all of three present they were more likely to be satisfied and make a purchase:

— The date they will receive the item (per delivery option). This is obviously the most important element to the user, especially if they have to be around to receive it. This is becoming standard, rather than an estimate such as stating '2-4 working days'.

— The cost of the delivery (per delivery option). Not surprisingly people are going to want to know how much their choice of delivery method will cost. If you offer an express service like next day delivery then be clear if this will cost extra compared to the default option. Users truly dislike it if they feel you're springing hidden charges on them.

— Extra: the date or time of dispatch (per product/order). If you dispatch items on the same day as the order then it's worth stating this, as this shows you are prompt. You can emphasise this with a countdown that shows the user how long they have to go until the cut-off time. If the dispatch date is notably further away then that is equally worth telling people up front so they can make an informed decision about ordering.

📖 Why showing the arrival date of a product is so important
go.mattish.com/ecom51

Delivery

Order in next **3 hours** for
dispatch today

Standard delivery Free | Receive by Saturday
Express delivery £10 | Receive by Thursday

Delivery

Standard delivery – 3-4 days
Express delivery – 1 day

BUTTONS

Buttons and CTAs have already been covered as an important part of landing pages (see page 24) and product pages (see page 78). And guess what? They're also an important part of your checkout flow.

In the checkout flow there should be no action more important than moving to the next step, so don't confuse users with other options. It's a simple one-way funnel; make it very clear how to proceed.

You will have already established a primary action style, so don't vary this. Use it for the button to enter the checkout and to move through any steps within it.

In my experience it even helps to keep the wording the same, so if the button from step one to two says 'continue', then use that for step two to three. You've created the expectation that this action takes the user forward, so make the most of it. You can alter the text when it's time to complete payment so the user is clear on what is happening—you should certainly do this if you're sending users to another site to pay.

How to use text in checkouts, including on buttons
go.mattish.com/ecom52

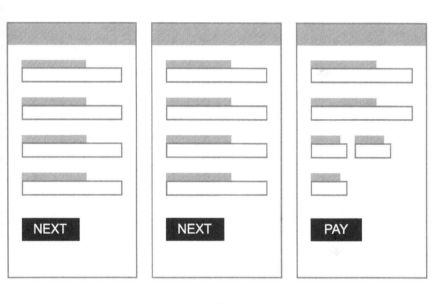

1   **2**   **3**

PAYMENT PROVIDERS

When you have a checkout flow you will need a partner service who deals with processing the payments. Some of these include Braintree, Adyen, Global Collect, and Stripe. Not all payment providers are the same, so it's worth understanding what yours offers and what their limitations are, as it can impact UX decisions:

— Does the provider require information to be collected first about the payee and then passed onto them? This will define what order steps need to come in.

— Do you have full control over the styling of the form fields, or will they be fixed by the payment provider? This could hamper how consistent you keep your experience.

— Will they use pop-ups/iframes/redirects to take the user to the payment step? This isn't ideal and can really break up a checkout process, causing users to question if it is secure.

Put simply, it comes down to control. How much are you able to completely customise the experience on your site and how much do they mandate for you? Work this out early before it scuppers any plans you may have.

📖

A good beginner's guide to understanding the role of payment providers **go.mattish.com/ecom53**

WORK THIS OUT **EARLY** BEFORE IT SCUPPERS YOUR PLANS

BASIC FORM USABILITY

Checkout flows are essentially a form filling exercise and no-one finds that particularly enjoyable. It's worth learning from the wealth of usability knowledge that has been built up around forms to your benefit. Here are three things you should certainly follow:

1. Put labels above—avoid having your field label sit on the left of the field itself. This layout can break on certain screen sizes and it's not always easy to see the relationship to the field if the gap gets too wide. Much better is to have the label sit above the field, where the relationship will be clear across all devices.

2. Show errors inline (after filling out)—a good error message is shown on the field itself. This way the user can instantly see where they went wrong, and not have to scan the page to discover the offending item. The error message shouldn't show up while the user is still typing: it's annoying and can cause them to think something is wrong when they just haven't finished typing.

3. Avoid placeholders in fields—placeholder text that sits inside a field has grown in popularity as designers look for ways to streamline their designs and save space. It can work for very small forms but on longer things like checkout flows it can make fields look filled in when they haven't been. It's a good idea to put any helper text outside the field rather than in it, otherwise as soon as the user starts typing that help disappears.

A great summary of several important form rules
go.mattish.com/ecom54

EMAIL

1

EMAIL

EMAIL

| nameemail.com | | ! |

Please check this is a valid email

2

EMAIL

| name | | ! |

Please check this is a valid email

EMAIL

Enter your work email

3

EMAIL

Enter your work email

MORE FORM USABILITY

Here are a few more tips on form design, that deal with some of the more subtle things you should consider:

1. Avoid dropdowns where possible—dropdown lists or select fields can be tempting to throw in when you have options you want users to choose from. However, when a list is short (fewer than about six options) you should break them out into a set of radio buttons. This way the user can easily see all the choices available and pick one with a single click or tap, avoiding the extra click/tap to open the menu. Save the dropdown for long lists with lots of options.

2. Nudge with field size—the size that you set your fields can help users see how much text they are expected to enter. For example you can help users realise they only need to enter a few characters in a post or zip code field by making it smaller than a phone number field. Equally if you need to use a text area for a user's message then the overall size of that will help indicate how many lines are expected of them.

3. Use autocomplete—this is more of a developer tip but make sure you utilise the browser autocomplete feature. If a user has it enabled it can save them typing in their name, email, phone number, and address—all things they're likely to have entered in the browser many times before. This is particularly useful for mobile devices as typing is harder on small screens so anything you can do to reduce it will be appreciated.

Some advanced things to try to make forms even quicker to fill
go.mattish.com/ecom55

CARD TYPE

| VISA | Mastercard | AMEX |

1

CARD TYPE

| Please choose ▼ |

POST CODE

| |

2

POST CODE

| |

EMAIL

| n| |
| first.lastname@email.com |

3

EMAIL

| first.lastname@email.com |

ARE YOU ASKING FOR TOO MUCH?

There's a simple way to help improve the conversion rate of a checkout flow and it's a method that works pretty reliably. Reduce the number of fields the user has to fill in.

The less work a user has to do, the more likely they are to go through with payment. The less daunting a checkout looks, the better.

With that in mind, is there anything in your checkout flow that you don't absolutely need to ask the user for them to be able to place their order? If you're not posting out items do you really need the whole address or would just a post code do? Are you ever going to use their phone number?

Do you really need to ask them how they found out about you? Smarter attribution tracking could cover this. In fact any kind of question about marketing or that isn't directly related to payment and delivery is a prime candidate to move outside of the checkout.

📖 Research suggesting the average checkout has twice as many fields as necessary **go.mattish.com/ecom56**

Name

[   ]

Email

[   ]

NEXT

Name

[   ]

Email

[   ]

How did you find us?

[   ]

Where else do you shop?

[   ]

NEXT

ORDER CONFIRMATION

There's a step that is easy to overlook in the checkout process. That's because it comes after you've got the user to part with their cash. Many sites will leave the order confirmation page as a simple 'thank you' message but this is a missed opportunity to help your customers and get more from them.

Firstly you can help by making sure that you clearly state what is going to happen next. Remind them when the item will be delivered and to what address (or where it will be available for collection). This allows them to double-check everything is happening as they expect.

You should also provide links to details about your cancellation and returns processes. Doing this (and repeating them in an email) will help prevent you having to deal with support messages from confused customers looking for this information.

Remember how we didn't want to bother the user at the start of the checkout process with creating an account? This is the point where you have more space to make clear the benefits they'll get in return for doing so. You just need to ask the user to set a password to add to their email address, which should feel like less work now it's separate from filling in other details. You can also ask them here if they'd like to sign up to any email newsletters.

Ideas and examples of extra content for the order confirmation page
go.mattish.com/ecom57

Your delivery

FAQs

Your order

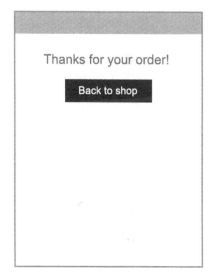

Thanks for your order!

Back to shop

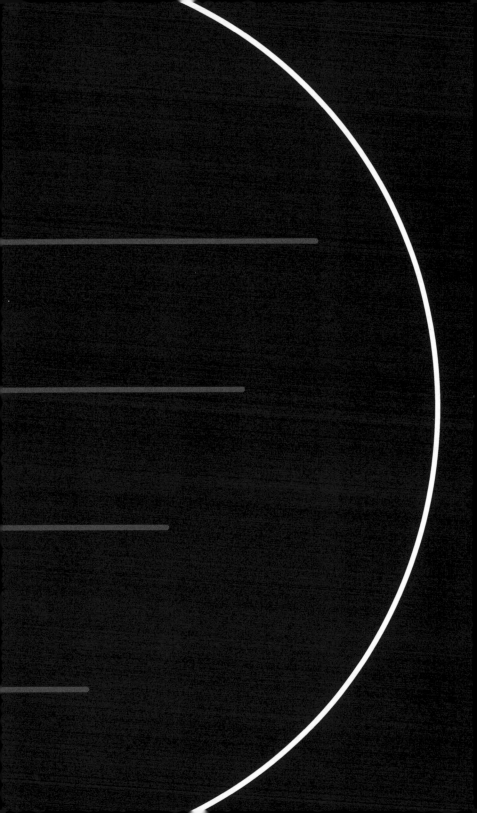

MORE

This section of the book is here for the advice that doesn't fit into the categories of the ecommerce funnel steps. These extra guidelines fall into two sub-categories: site-wide considerations and content pages.

SITE-WIDE

These considerations can potentially apply across every step in the flow and any other pages you may have. They are worth establishing for your website to maintain consistency and are often referred to by developers as global elements. It will depend on the scale of your website as to how many of these elements you need.

CONTENT PAGES

Content-led ecommerce brands are those that generate their own editorial as a way of attracting users to visit (often referred to as inbound marketing). Some companies will treat this as a completely separate section like a blog. In truth these pages effectively sit 'on top' of a standard ecommerce funnel and thus act as an alternative form of landing page. Content can also include 'about' pages or information pages that are not directly sales related but do offer a space to give more detail about the company, a product, or a line of products.

This chapter covers a final nine guidelines for helping your ecommerce website function as a satisfying whole.

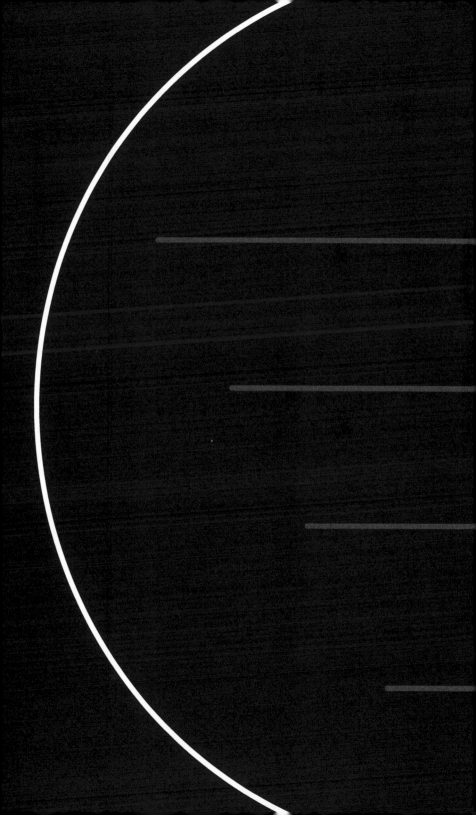

CONTACT METHODS

No-one knows when they're going to get stuck. Users can run into issues on any page of your site, and whether they are struggling to find their way around or have a pressing question about a product, you should make it easy for them to get in touch.

If you have a staffed phone line, then you should show this off as it builds trust that you are a legitimate brand and helps less-confident web users see there is a safety net. Live chat can be another great tool for allowing users to contact a real person (without the call queues).

The best place to put a phone number or 'customer services' link is generally in the header which is an obvious part of every page. You may lack header space on a mobile so put your contact link at the top of the footer. Mobile users are already holding a phone so make the number a telephone link to enable them to call with a tap.

Live chat buttons tend to be fixed to the bottom of the browser window, which is fine as long as they aren't too big and don't get in the way by opening as soon as the user lands on the site.

Ideas for great ecommerce customer service
go.mattish.com/ecom58

LOGO 0800 123 4567 | Contact

LOGO

SITE NAVIGATION

How do you arrange the navigation of a site with hundreds or thousands of products and lots of categories? What's the best way to help users to find what they're after? The answer might surprise you.

You don't need to spend ages deciding which items to show and which to strip out. Instead define a sensible set of top level navigation items (like departments of a shop) and on the next tier show all the product categories within that.

This can create what's known as a mega menu, sometimes filling most of the screen on desktop and providing a lot of options. It might seem like too much but you never know the exact thing your users are after and as long as it's alphabetically ordered they'll be able to quickly reach what they need. For mobile the menus usually take over the screen anyway but you might need an extra tier in the hierarchy to fit everything in.

Not sure if a product type should live in one department or another? Then you should put them in both. There's no harm in repeating because if you're not sure how to categorise something then there's bound to be users who don't either.

Examples showing how mega menus are only getting bigger on desktop **go.mattish.com/ecom59**

YOU NEVER KNOW THE

EXACT THING

YOUR USERS ARE AFTER

PREFERENCES

There's some information that users can find themselves entering repeatedly on an ecommerce site in order to make a purchase. If you're smart then you can save them from having to do this.

Clothing size is a good example of something a user must specify but when they've done it once, you can default to it on other products. A growing number of brands use fit finders which get the user to fill out some details about themselves in order to give size recommendations across the site.

You can also store their searches in a cookie which can pre-fill user preferences when they revisit the site. For example if they're looking for holiday accommodation, the dates of their trip are probably going to remain constant so you can use what was previously entered. Of course they might want to change their parameters but an educated guess is always going to have more chance of being right than a blank field.

Little things like this will help your brand feel smoother and less hassle than going elsewhere and if users create an account on your site, any number of preferences can be stored for future visits.

A look at how a couple of fit finders work
go.mattish.com/ecom60

Start date

| 20 May |

End date

| 25 May |

Guests

| 4 people |

Location

| New York |

Start date

| Please choose |

End date

| Please choose |

Guests

| Please choose |

Location

| Please choose |

COLLECTION

A growing number of ecommerce websites offer users the ability to collect their order rather than have it delivered. It's very useful for users who aren't at home and can't get delivery to work. There are two main ways to do this and one involves more complexity than the other.

The easiest approach is to add collection as an alternative to delivery in the checkout. Get the user to enter their location and show them options for where they can pick up their order, and when it will be ready. It's also important to show the pick up location's opening hours—this data often comes from integrating with a delivery company.

The more complex approach is to integrate the option to collect into the rest of the site. This is usually done by brands who have bricks and mortar stores as it allows users to check if an item is in stock in a specific shop.

The complexity arises on many sites where the user specifies whether they want to collect at the product page level. If they have multiple products in their order and aren't diligent they can end up with some products ordered for delivery and some for collection (or a 'mixed' basket). To avoid this the earliest I recommend letting the user specify collection or delivery is at the basket stage so it applies to the whole order.

A look at the problems of a mixed basket
go.mattish.com/ecom61

THERE ARE TWO WAYS TO DO THIS AND ONE IS MORE COMPLEX THAN THE OTHER

MORE

COUNTRY & CURRENCY

If you're selling to users in other countries then you need to help them feel confident about making a purchase. Internationalisation can seem like a scary thing to approach but whilst translating copy is tough, allowing a user to set their country and a currency is relatively straight forward. You can find plug-ins that allow users to set this for most ecommerce platforms.

Specifying their country helps users know that their order will reach them, and that they will be quoted the right costs for taxes and shipping. Users seeing prices in their native currency are also much more likely to feel at home on the site and won't have to keep doing conversion sums to work out if they can afford something. It's trivial for a machine to do this task so don't put it upon your users.

You can automatically detect where users are coming from through their IP address but you should allow the user to edit this themselves too. IP detection isn't always accurate and there can be cases where users are abroad but intend to order to their home country.

The standard places to provide the link to specify country and currency is the top right on desktop, or the footer on mobile. It's a good idea to display the setting in an overlay window, so the user can make the change whilst keeping their place in the ecommerce funnel.

📖 The benefits of displaying prices in the user's local currency
go.mattish.com/ecom62

YOUR SETTINGS

Country

United Kingdom ▼

Currency

£ GBP ▼

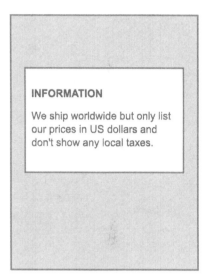

INFORMATION

We ship worldwide but only list our prices in US dollars and don't show any local taxes.

MORE

YOUR CMS

Whether it's Shopify, SquareSpace, Magento, or something else, a Content Management System (CMS) can save you a lot of time in coding. Despite this, each platform will have its own limitations on what you can do with your site.

If you use a CMS then you should understand how it is structured and what can be achieved with it. It can affect a variety of things, from how search is displayed, the flexibility to customise filters, the structure of the checkout process, and how basket functionality like promo codes and vouchers work.

Another thing that forms a part of the design of your site but is often overlooked, is the URL structure. Does your CMS allow for you to put page types, categories, and product names in the URL? Or is it all just a messy query string? Cleaner, human readable URLs allow you to create a structure that is scalable whilst making it easy to identify pages in tools like Google Analytics.

Knowing the tools and the medium you work in is important for any designer. Get a developer to help you understand if it all gets too technical. Of course if you have a custom-built site then it should be possible to build anything you want, although it will probably be more work.

📖 Comparison of five of the biggest ecommerce
CMS platforms **go.mattish.com/ecom63**

KNOW THE TOOLS AND THE MEDIUM YOU WORK IN

EDITORIAL CONTENT

The ecommerce funnel is a fairly simple affair but you might want to create additional content to draw in more users. Relevant editorial content can help showcase your USP and build you up as an authority on a subject. There is one effective way to feature this content in the buying flow and one that could harm your sales.

Think of this content as sitting alongside landing pages at the top of the funnel. Generally it is in the form of articles to draw users in from organic searches or social media. These content pages should then link through to featured products and category pages. Your content should be related to what you sell (even if it isn't specifically about that) and it should be obvious where to find your products on that page. Not all users will be interested in clicking but make it easy for those that are.

To avoid harming your conversion rate don't put links off to the articles on the product pages. You don't want intriguing content cannibalising users' interest and distracting them away from the main focus of the product page, which is to sell. This is unless you know there's lots to explain about the product and there is a long lead time before users buy.

The content marketing process should be a one-way street sending people from the editorial through to shop. If you have fixed information you want to supply to users such as how your product is made, then provide it in the form of pop-ups so they don't leave the product page.

Design options for presenting products on article pages
go.mattish.com/ecom64

The best products for going to new places

SHOP

SHOP

BUY

INFORMATION PAGES

Do you have lots you want to say about your brand or an element of your service? It's possible there are things to explain about your USP or at the very least the company itself (generally in the form of an 'about' page). If it's something that applies across a lot of your products then it makes sense to have a separate page to link to, so you can go into more detail.

Don't make this information page a wall of text. If you've got something interesting to tell your audience, then make it interesting to consume. If in doubt decide on three key points you want them to remember, and focus on these.

You should illustrate with imagery and break the text up into short, scannable sections as people don't tend to read long blocks of copy when they're in shopping mode. Even something fairly dry like delivery information can be made quick and easy to dip into.

Examples of effective about pages and the key elements you can include **go.mattish.com/ecom65**

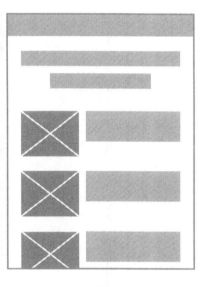

DO YOU WANT TO LOOK LUXURY?

There's a shortcut to looking high-end and luxury in the ecommerce space and it doesn't require complex work. It does however require a good eye and an appreciation of graphic design.

High-end sites generally go for only one or two typefaces, with only a few variations in size and style (often with minimal use of bold and italics). The colour palette is usually restrained to muted colours, or even just black and white with an optional accent colour. White space is used liberally to give a feeling of prestige and to show the content isn't packed in. Finally the imagery will be large, high quality, and given centre-stage.

Of course there are other things that count towards a luxurious experience, like speed of page loading and a lack of unnecessary extra steps in the user journey. But users will judge you quickest by first impressions and how the visual design comes across.

Consciously or not, the surface design matters to users and should be congruent with the products available for sale. If you products cost a lot, then the design of the website had better back this up.

More detail on how to look luxury (and how not to)
go.mattish.com/ecom66

THE DESIGN OF THE WEBSITE HAD

BETTER
BACK
THIS
UP

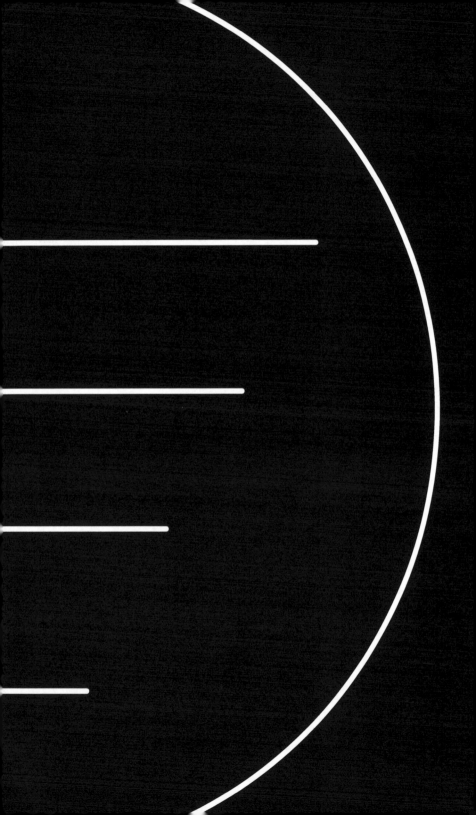

GLOSSARY

Attention ratio
The ratio of all links on a page to the the most important link you want users to choose (which should always be one). A high ratio is usually a warning sign you have too much on your page.

Attribution tracking
Analytics that tracks what users have clicked to find your website.

Banner ads
In-page advertising on websites.

Bounce rate
Browsing sessions which result in the user leaving the site having only viewed one page. Expressed as a percentage against total number of visiting users.

Carousel
An interactive element on a webpage which contains several different images (often with text), which move horizontally into view.

Click-through
When a user clicks a link on the page, generally moving onto the next step in the funnel.

CMS
Stands for Content Management System and is where website administrators are able to edit the text and images on a website without needing to code.

Copy
Any kind of written content but often that which has been written for marketing purposes.

CTA
Stands for Call To Action and refers to the text that users must click or tap to complete an action. This text often lives in a button.

Filter categories
A grouping of filter options, e.g. brand, size, colour.

Filter values
A set of filter options within a category, e.g. for the category of colour the values could be red, blue, yellow.

Iframe
A module containing content and code from another website.

IP address
An identifier for each computer/device on the web.

Query string
The text which comes after a '?' in a URL and contains parameters defining the content shown on the page.

SEO
Stands for Search Engine Optimisation and means methods used to get a higher ranking on search engines (mainly Google).

The fold
An imaginary line on a website marked out by the height of your browser window. Elements are then said to be either above or below the fold.

Tooltip
A message which appears when a cursor hovers over an icon or link (or appears when tapped for mobile devices).

User testing
A way to find out how easy to use something is by testing it with real people, who are asked to complete tasks.

USP
Stands for Unique Selling Point and is a marketing term for what makes your brand/product different.

Visitor recordings
Videos of real users moving around a website, showing where they scroll and click/tap.

AFTERWORD

Thanks for reading! I hope you found it useful and gained some advice that you can apply to whatever you're working on. With a bit of luck this book will be a reference you can return to in future.

If you liked what you read and got something from it, please do leave a review on Amazon (link: **go.mattish.com/ecom67**). For self-published authors like me, those reviews make all the difference in getting sales when you don't have the machinery of a publishing house, and are massively appreciated. And of course please tell friends and colleagues.

If you want to discuss something in more detail or critique parts of the book, then email me on **matt@mattish.com**. I'm always happy to explore and debate the ideas here.

You can hire me to give a workshop on the content in this book, illustrated with loads of real world examples. There's more information on my website.

I don't have plans to make another edition of this so any future ecommerce UX advice will be made available on my site, free of charge. You can get the latest content as soon as it's written (and a few other bonuses) at **mattish.com/newsletter**.

ACKNOWLEDGEMENTS

As ever my biggest thanks go to my partner Jen, for sharing an office with me, being supportive of my ideas, and for being my occasional editor. Her honesty, patience, and better grasp of English have hugely improved my writing skills over the years.

A big thanks must also go to my good friend Nam, who has done a great job of designing this book (for the second time) and passing on his print expertise. You should hire him if you have a book you want to look sharp—check out **nam-design.co.uk**.

Thank you to everyone who has attended all of my ecommerce UX workshops, particularly the early ones. Smart student questioning helped the content improve, and in turn helped strengthen this book.

Finally, cheers to all the folks on my mailing list for engaging with my UX content, especially those who have test read the early versions of this book, and provided feedback.

Made in the USA
Middletown, DE
08 March 2020